M000307058

How to Know the Individual Will of God

By Charles L. Surrett

Surrett Family Publications

Kings Mountain, North Carolina

2015

ISBN 978-0-9789331-3-5

Forward

During my doctoral studies I became acquainted with the book by Garry Friesen entitled, *Decision Making and the Will of God*. It alarmed me that the traditional view of the individual will of God would be so strongly challenged, and I felt that a modern-day defense of the long-held view might be needed. It was my intention to write simply a positive presentation of the individual will of God for my doctoral dissertation, but my faculty advisor told me that I had to go "head-to-head" with Friesen's exegesis. While I do not enjoy being confrontational, by following my advisor's stipulation I greatly strengthened my conviction in the matter. The more I looked into the Hebrew language of the Old Testament and the Greek of the New Testament, the more convinced I became that the traditional view of the will of God is right.

While the lengths to which I go to disprove Friesen's theory may seem tedious and repetitious to some readers, I have become convinced that there is no doubt that the case presented here is true to the Scriptures. It is unfortunate that Friesen's view has become popular in some academic circles, influencing young ministerial students. It is my hope that those who have an appreciation for the exegesis of Scripture will not so readily reject the fact of a specific, knowable will of God for each individual Christian.

It has taken me twenty-five years since doing the initial work to finally get around to publishing this study. Perhaps that is well, because I have had many opportunities to put these principles into practice in my life and ministry. And, without necessarily planning it that way, I see that the book has unfolded as a representation of my own experience, with the beginning part focusing on the exegetical, and the latter part focusing on the practical, aspects of knowing the will of God.

I have now spent more than fifty years in the ministry, including the years of formal preparation, and it has been a great assurance to me that God has a specific plan for my life and service for Him. Knowing that I was in the place where God wanted me to be at specific times helped me to get through some of the difficulties I faced as a pastor. It has been a wonderful life that God has planned for me, and vastly superior to any plans I might have made for myself.

I have also now been married for over fifty years, and it has been a sweet comfort for these decades to know that God gave me the one who is "good, acceptable, and perfect" for me! She has been my help meet, cheerleader, friend, lover, companion, proofreader, source of encouragement, *etc., etc., etc.* She is a great wife, mother, grandmother, and great-grandmother. And therefore I dedicate this book to the one who is God's perfect choice for me, Rosanne Marie (Van Pelt) Surrett, whom I love dearly.

Chuck Surrett

Table of Contents

Chapter 1

Introduction

The purpose of this book is to prove that God has a specific, individual will for each Christian, and to reveal how that will can be discerned.

The fact that God has a specific will has been challenged by Garry Friesen, in *Decision Making and the Will of God*. Friesen's work demands that the "traditional" view (defended here) be refined, and that the fallacies of his thinking be refuted. In essence, Friesen "poisons the well" of logic by stating that the Bible illustrations of the individual leading of God are not normative (applicable to all believers), since the process of writing Scripture was incomplete when each event took place. However, this type of reasoning would eliminate every Bible illustration of any truth from being considered normative. In reality, illustrations can be considered normative when reinforced by clear Biblical instruction, as will be seen in the case of individual guidance.

Also, Friesen claims to avoid subjectivity in his search for Biblical wisdom in decision making, but he fails to fulfill that claim by relying upon internal "wisdom." The contention here is that God *does* work within the hearts of believers, making inner peace an indicator of His will. Friesen presents a good system of using the Bible in decision making, but his view can more properly be seen as preliminary to the traditional process. That is, the "inner peace" method follows the Scripture search, in discerning God's will. If the decision is not yet made once the Bible has been consulted, other steps can still be taken.

Friesen is not alone in claiming that there is no specific, individual will of God for every believer. The popular evangelical author, Jay Adams, takes a similar position. Adams clearly states this in *More Than Redemption*: "The first, and absolutely fundamental, fact to zealously maintain is that there is no way to know God's will and receive His guidance apart from the Scriptures."[1] Describing a hypothetical case study of "Herb," who is trying to decide whether he should marry "Jane" or "Betty," Adams says:

> If, indeed, all other things are equal, and there are no biblical principles that prohibit marriage to Jane or Betty, then Herb may conclude that (in the sense of God's directive will revealed in the Scriptures) marriage to *either* (emphasis his) woman is a legitimate option. It is neither right nor wrong, biblically, to marry (or not marry) either one. . . . Herb should recognize that he would not be wrong in marrying either Jane or Betty."[2]

Adams then adds, "Thus, Herb has the right, within the options that God has left him, to decide for Betty . . . over Jane *purely on a preferential basis* (emphasis his).[3] He further concludes that:

---

[1] Jay Adams, <u>More Than Redemption</u>, 28.
[2] Ibid.
[3] Ibid., 29.

7

In an absolute or ultimate sense, then, the Christian cannot talk about "God's will" *before* (emphasis his) the fact in a multi-option context. He can only say, generally, "I see that it is God's will to marry a girl *like* (emphasis his) Jane or Betty.[4]

Adams thinks that the will of God concerning marriage can only be known *after the fact*, assuming that ". . . whatever comes to pass is His eternal (or decretive) will."[5] This is what will be called in this study the *determinative* will of God. In other words, according to Adams, since Herb *actually married* Betty, he could *then* know that marriage to her was God's will. Obviously, in the view of Adams, believers cannot make these types of decisions with assurance beforehand that God has led them to these choices. Herb's marriage could turn out to be a disaster, and he would fatalistically conclude that it is God's will for him to suffer in that unhappiness, but there would have been no way for him to avoid the disaster!

The will of God has been a misunderstood concept to many Christians. After hearing the subject heralded for decades by preachers of the Bible, many believers still have a nebulous view that appears quite impractical, to say nothing of unbiblical. And, as has been noted already, there are even those who deny that God

---

[4] Ibid., 30.
[5] Ibid., 28.

has a knowable plan that is unique to each individual.[6] Therefore, it is important to discover whether, in fact, God has such a plan, and if so, how to discern what it is. The following words express the approach that this study will take:

> Can you think of a father who has no will or plan for the life of his son? Can you imagine a mother who has no clear will or definite ambition for her daughter? Can you imagine a man who has no special desire or pattern in the one he chooses to be his wife? Can you conceive of a king or ruler who has no will or desire or law to conduct of his people? A captain who has no plan for his soldiery? An employer who has no plan or pattern to guide the labor of his workers? A shepherd who has no object in view for his sheep? A vine that has no positive purpose in its branches? If so, then you may also think that God does not have a plan for your life, for every one of these symbols is used in the Bible to represent the relation the Christian bears to His (*sic*) Lord.[7]

Justification of the Study

Believers in Christ want to make wise decisions and should take advantage of the provision of God's wisdom available

---

[6] Philip Yancey, "Finding the Will of God: No Magic Formulas," Christianity Today, 27, No. 14 (September 16, 1983): 23-24.
[7] G. Christian Weiss, The Perfect Will of God, 15.

to them. Since man is accountable to God for the decisions he makes, then man must know the very best way to make decisions. In recent decades, the idea that God gives inward guidance to individual believers has been challenged. A persuasive case has been built by Friesen for the argument that Christians have only the Word of God and wisdom to rely upon in decision making.[8] Thus, it seems important to examine the teachings of Scripture on the subject. The final conclusion must be made upon Biblical, not pragmatic, bases.

Definitions of Terms

The aspects of God's will. The will of God is, in simple terms, that which He desires to see accomplished. The Greek words, θελω and βουλομαι, are the most frequently-used verbs for "to will" in the New Testament. They express desire, with varying degrees of certainty, depending upon individual contexts. M. Blaine Smith tries to build a case for a clear-cut difference in the usage of these two words, to distinguish between the sovereign will of God and that which He merely desires to see accomplished. Smith maintains that θελω is used every time the New Testament stresses man's responsibility,[9] and that βουλομαι always refers to the sovereign aspect of God's will.[10] However, disagreement with

---

[8] Garry Friesen, Decision Making and the Will of God, 82-83.
[9] M. Blaine Smith, Knowing God's Will, 21.
[10] Ibid., 21-22.

this hypothesis can be found in the Greek lexicons of Arndt and Gingrich,[11] as well as Vine.[12] More accurately, it can be said that θελω and its noun form, θελημα, are the terms most often used to refer to man's responsibility for discerning the will of God. Clearly, however, God has both a determinative and non-determinative will, and His non-determinative will is both general and specific.

God's determinative will. There are some elements of God's will that are sovereign, which He will accomplish, regardless of man's responses. This will also be referred to here as the determinative will of God. The logical progression of this concept is stated by A. H. Strong:

> Foreknowledge implies fixity, and fixity implies decree. From eternity God foresaw all the events of the universe as fixed and certain. This fixity and certainty could not have had its ground either in blind fate or in the variable wills of men, since neither of these had any existence. It could have had its ground in nothing outside the divine mind, for in eternity nothing existed besides the divine mind. But for this fixity there must have been a cause; if anything in the future was fixed, something must have

---

[11] BAG, 4th rev. ed., s. v. "Βουλομαι,"145.
[12] W. E. Vine, An Expository Dictionary of New Testament Words, vol. 4, 222.

fixed it. This fixity could have had its ground only in the plan and purpose of God. In fine, if God foresaw the future as certain, it must have been because there was something in himself which made it certain, or, in other words, because he had decreed it.[13]

God's non-determinative will. The non-determinative will of God is that which He desires to accomplish through the means of man's voluntary cooperation. This is seen in I Timothy 2:4, where God is "wishing" (θελει) for all men to become saved. Salvation, however, is not the universal experience of mankind. Another example is II Peter 3:9, where God is described as One Who is not "wishing" (Βουλομενος) that any should perish. Both of these Scripture passages reveal to us that there is an aspect of God's will that could be considered as an unfulfilled wish, which is dependent upon man's response to God's will.[14] It is in the non-determinative area that the bulk of this study will concentrate. This is the aspect of God's will that man needs most to comprehend and obey.

God's general will. This term will be used here to refer to man's life as God has commanded. This is given to us in the Bible, and is the same for all people. The individual details come into

---

[13] Augustus Hopkins Strong, Systematic Theology, 356.

[14] These passages also demonstrate the previously-mentioned position that the distinctions between θελω and βουλομαι have to be made primarily on the basis of context.

account only after the general will of God has been considered and obeyed. In other words, the universally-revealed truths have a logical priority over individual leading, and God's general will cannot be superseded or contradicted by His specific will.

The Internalization of God's Will

It will be contended here that God does, in fact, work within the individual Christian to provide specific leadership. This fact is frequently referred to in Scripture, even though some object that such internalization is "subjective."[15] Exegetical considerations of several Old and New Testament passages will reveal this recurring theme.

Outline of the Study

This study will be structured in a form that is intended to build logically and progressively toward the forced conclusion that there is a definite, specific will of God for every individual, which can be known with certainty. Chapter two will deal with the two aspects of God's will on which Bible-believers agree. First, a study of the sovereign, or determinative, will of God will be briefly undertaken. Next, the Bible methods of determining the "general" will of God will be noted. These methods will give the important Biblical steps that apply to decision making in general and will illustrate principles of searching the Scripture for

---

[15] Friesen, 130.

decisions. The third chapter will deal with the specific will of God, proving from the Old Testament that it is a Bible concept. Chapter four will provide exegesis of pertinent New Testament Scriptures relating to the specific will of God. The next portion will give a suggested process for determining the specific will of God, as illustrated in Genesis 24. Chapter six will show how God often reveals His will by saying, "No" to man. Chapter seven will reveal some general application principles, chapter eight will list six pointers to the will of God, and chapter nine will summarize the material.

To save the repetitious use of time and space, two major exegetical reference books will be abbreviated in the footnotes. BAG refers to the Greek Lexicon of Bauer, Arndt, and Gingrich. TWOT is the Hebrew Lexicon entitled, *Theological Wordbook of the Old Testament*.

Chapter 2

Two Aspects of God's Will

There are two aspects of the will of God that are undisputed. Proponents of both the "wisdom" method and the "peace" method of decision making acknowledge the reality of the determinative, as well as the general, will of God. It will be beneficial to note some areas of agreement between the two positions, before focusing on their differences.

The Determinative Will

Attention will be directed now to the fact of the sovereign, or determinative, will of God. This section is intended to demonstrate that God has a sovereign will, and that it affects much of man's life, especially his sanctification. However, it will also be seen that God has limited Himself by giving man the freedom to make moral choices. Some Biblical examples of this will be given, to show that man actually has the power to oppose the will of God. This power, of course, will increase man's accountability to God.

The determinative will of God has been defined here as that which God purposes to accomplish, regardless of man's response. It is as certain as if already enacted in history, just because God wills it this way. It is a part of the sovereign aspect of God's nature, which illustrates His absolute control in creation. Certain events and circumstances were decreed beforehand by God, and the decrees themselves guarantee the certainty of their fulfillment. One author states it this way: "All things are included in God's plan, but some things He causes and others He permits."[16] It is the causative part of God's plan that is here called the determinative, or sovereign, will of God.

Proofs of Sovereignty

Scriptural examples. A detailed study of the sovereign is beyond the scope of this book, but some evidences will be given. A few of the areas in which God exercises sovereignty are noted here: (1) the stability of God's Word and of His universe [Psalm 119:89-91]; (2) national circumstances [Acts 17:26]; (3) human life and its duration [Job 14:5]; (4) the means of human death [John 21:29]; and (5) certain acts of men [Genesis 50:20].[17] In missionary endeavors, the Apostle Paul's will was overruled by God's sovereign will (Acts 16:6-9), but that also served to guide Paul into God's individual will for his ministry. In fact, many aspects of Christian service result from determination, as is seen from Ephesians 2:10: ". . . good works, which God hath before ordained that we should walk in them."[18] Using the illustration of the potter and clay, Paul rhetorically asserts that men have not resisted God's sovereign will (Romans 9:19-21). The determinative will of God plays an essential role in the salvation and sanctification of believers, as indicated by the description of Romans 8:28-30, where predestination results in believers being conformed to the image of Christ:

---

[16] Emery H. Bancroft, Elemental Theology, 69.
[17] A. H. Strong, Systematic Theology, 355.

And we know that all things work together for good to them that love God, to them who are the called according to his purpose. For whom he did foreknow, he also did predestinate to be conformed to the image of his Son, that he might be the firstborn among many brethren. Moreover whom he did predestinate, them he also called: and whom he called, them he also justified: and whom he justified, them he also glorified.

Ephesians 1:4-6 further verifies this truth, which results in believers becoming "holy and without blame" and "accepted in the beloved":

According as he hath chosen us in him before the foundation of the world, that we should be holy and without blame before him in love: having predestinated us unto the adoption of children by Jesus Christ to himself, according to the good pleasure of his will, to the praise of the glory of his grace, wherein he hath made us accepted in the beloved.

The national election of Israel is another illustration of the determinative will of God. Isaiah 45:4 describes Israel as God's elect, intimating that God will accomplish His purpose, despite Israel's lack of spiritual understanding (". . . though thou has not known me").

Evidences of Divine Self-Limitation

Having noted that God is sovereign, and that aspects of His will are determinative, it is important to balance the picture

17

with a recognition of the freedom God gives man in moral choices. This freedom is not contradictory to God's nature, since it comes from a Self-limitation that was not externally imposed upon God. Man's will is ". . . the soul's power to choose between motives and to direct its subsequent activity according to the motive thus chosen."[19] This power is granted by God as a voluntary limitation of His own sovereignty. The obvious consequence is the possibility that man's choices might oppose the desires of God.

Bible Examples. There are two quite clear examples of God's Self-limitation that should be noted. In I Timothy 2:4, it is God's will for ". . . all men to be saved, and to come unto the knowledge of the truth." In II Peter 3:9, God is ". . . not willing that any should perish, but that all should come to repentance." These are two examples of something that God *desires* to happen, that most often will *not* happen. In most cases concerning repentance and salvation, man's freedom is exercised in opposition to God's will (Matthew 7:13-14). Thus, it is not inappropriate to conclude that God has an unfulfilled wish with regard to the universal salvation of mankind.

Human accountability. Of course, when man opposes God, he heightens his own accountability to God and must be prepared to face the consequences of his affections and actions.[20]

---

[19] A. H. Strong, 504.
[20] Ibid., 509.

When God limits Himself to giving man freedom, then man must respond by choosing to agree with the revealed desires of God. In this light, it is fitting to state that the determinative will of God includes a revelation of His non-determinative will. The statement of Acts 22:14 explains that God chose for man to know what choices God wants man to make: "The God of our fathers hath chosen thee, that thou shouldest know his will. . . . "

To review this brief notation of the determinative will of God, it is defined as that aspect of His will which is causative, which will be accomplished regardless of man's response. It involves many aspects of human history, including the salvation and sanctification of men. To balance that, God has limited Himself by giving man a free will, which presents the possibility that man's choices might oppose God's will. Therefore, man's accountability to God is increased because of the freedom of choice. A truly Biblical view will account for both the sovereignty of God and the will of man.

The General Will

Objectivity

The general will of God is that which He desires for all people. It is revealed in the written Word of God, and much of it gives the same requirements for both believers and unbelievers. There are also many commandments for Christians that place all believers under identical requirements, which do not necessarily apply to the unsaved. In addition, God has given to all certain Bible principles which aid in the decision making process, as further evidence of the general will of God. This must be taken into account when believers make decisions.

> Some earnest people have magnified the inner light and leading of the Holy Spirit to the neglect of the Word which He gave, and through which He still works on human hearts. This is a great mistake and the prolific parent of all kinds of evil.[21]

Direct commandments. Morgan says that ". . . the supreme subject of Scriptures is the will of God."[22] There are multitudes of commandments from God that reveal His will for His creation. For example, God commands ". . . all men every where to repent (Acts 17:30)." This is an unqualified statement, so there are to be no exceptions. The obvious conclusion is that every individual who refuses to repent is out of the will of God. The book, *His Will*, lists 206 different categories of Bible commandments, each of which has numerous verses with specific details.[23] Thus, there are literally hundreds of commandments from God in the Bible.

Christians must be familiar with Bible commandments because: (1) they will be judged according to them [Romans 2:12] and (2) the specific will of God can never contradict His general will. That is, no Christian will have specific leading that is not in

---

[21] F. B. Meyer, The Secret of Guidance, 121.
[22] G. Campbell Morgan, God's Perfect Will, 35.
[23] C. M. and M. J. Ellinwood, His Will, 11-13.

agreement with the Bible. An example of God's general will is seen in I Thessalonians 4:3: "For this is the will of God, even your sanctification, that ye should abstain from fornication." This is stated as the universal will of God for believers.

Dispensational considerations. The commandments of God's Word must be interpreted in the light of dispensational considerations. For example, virtually all Christian scholars today understand that believers are no longer to bring animal sacrifices to God, even though they were commanded to do so in the Law (Leviticus 16).[24] Dispensational interpretation has been variously termed "literal," "grammatical-historical," "normal," and "plain" interpretation. It signifies taking the Bible at its face value, allowing for obvious figures of speech to be understood.[25]

Although there are non-dispensationalists who claim to take the Bible literally, they do not appear to follow the principle consistently, especially when it pertains to the interpretation of prophecy.[26] O. T. Allis has acknowledged that amillennialists differ from premillennialists because ". . . they do not interpret the Bible with the same degree of literalness. . . . " as do the premillennialists.[27] Therefore, a dispensational view of God's

---

[24] Charles Caldwell Ryrie, Dispensationalism Today, 127-131.
[25] Ibid., 86-87.
[26] Ibid., 89.
[27] Oswald T. Allis, Prophecy and the Bible, 17.

21

Word helps the Christian to understand which Bible commands apply today, and which do not.

Cultural interpretation. To a lesser degree, cultural considerations affect Bible interpretation. There are some commandments that apply only to certain cultures, which are not binding upon all believers today. The command in I Thessalonians 5:26 to "Greet all the brethren with an holy kiss" needs to be seen in its proper cultural setting.

> In the Church the kiss was the pledge of brotherhood; those who exchanged it declared themselves members of one family. . . . Of course, its only value was as the natural expression of brotherly love; where the natural expression of such love was not kissing, but the grasping of the hand, or the friendly inclination of the head, the Christian kiss ought to have died a natural death.[28]

The same thing could be said of Jesus' instructions to His disciples to wash each other's feet (John 13:14). It was a common matter of Oriental hospitality,[29] and also an "example" (John 13:15) of humility and servitude. If this were not a symbolic act, Jesus would not have needed to ask if the disciples knew what He had done unto them (verse 12), for they certainly knew that He

---

[28] W. Robertson Nicoll, ed., The Expositor's Bible, vol. 6, 539.
[29] Charles F. Pfeiffer, and Everett F. Harrison, eds., The Wycliffe Bible Commentary, 1102.

had washed their feet. He was asking if they understood the symbolism of the act.

It would be wrong to assume that God wants all Christians of every culture to practice the kiss of brotherly love and footwashing as church ordinances, but the principles of friendly affection and humble servitude ought to be demonstrated in each cultural setting.

Principles. In addition to direct commandments of Scripture, understood in their dispensational and cultural contexts, the Christian must give careful heed to the *principles* of God's Word, which will aid him in decision making. Just as the commandments cannot be exhaustively listed here, neither can all the applicable principles of Christian living. However, a brief look at Romans 14:1-15:3 is helpful in comprehending the subject.

The section deals with doubtful things, or areas of personal application wherein two Bible believers may differ with each other and both be right. Since many Jews lived in Rome in Paul's day, it is likely that the church there had a sizeable mixture of Jews among the Gentiles.[30] Such a mixture normally resulted in the Jewish believers attempting to bind Gentile Christians to the customs that were typically Jewish.[31] Paul wrote to encourage the

---

[30] Albert Barnes, <u>Barnes' Notes on the New Testament</u>, 653.
[31] Ibid.

Christians to maintain an attitude of graciousness toward those Godly believers with whom they disagreed.

The principle subject of dispute was concerning *meats* and *days*. The converted Jew, retaining a veneration for the law of Moses, abstained from certain meats, and was observant of certain days; while the converted Gentile, understanding that the Christian religion laid him under no obligations to such ceremonial points, had no regard to either. It appears, further, that mutual censures and uncharitable judgments prevailed among them, and that brotherly love and mutual forbearance did not generally prevail.[32]

Internal convictions. With such a background, the first principle Paul notes is that individual believers must avoid judging and despising one another when their personal applications differ (verses 1-3). This is an important principle for life that should help in the making of all decisions whose conclusions are not forced by the Scriptures. Second, Paul stresses the importance of individual convictions (verse 5). "Persuaded" is πληροφορεισθω, which means, "let him be convinced fully."[33] This refers to an internal

---

[32] Adam Clarke, Romans to the Revelations, vol. 2 of The New Testament of Our Lord and Savior Jesus Christ, 150.

[33] BAG, 4th rev. ed., s. v. "πληροφορεω," 676.

conviction ("in his own mind"), which is not necessarily the same for each individual.

Motives. A third principle in this chapter is found in verses 6-8: whatever is done should be done as unto the Lord. In verses 10-12, the reader is reminded that all will give account to God the Judge. The fifth principle is the warning against putting a "stumblingblock" in another's way (verse 13). This word is σκανδαλον, which originally referred to the part of a trap to which the bait was attached, and eventually was used for the trap itself.[34] The conclusion is that a Christian ought not to do anything that might ensnare another spiritually. In verses 15-17 Paul teaches the principle that spiritual things ("the kingdom of God") are more important than physical things ("meat and drink"). The seventh principle, taken from verse nineteen, is that believers ought to seek to "edify" (οικοδομης = "the promotion of spiritual growth")[35] each other.

Failure is sin. The chapter concludes with the declaration that ". . . whatsoever is not of faith is sin (verse 23)." The word for "sin" is αμαρτια, whose etymology means "a missing of the mark."[36] Therefore, the individual who wants to

---

[34] W. E. Vine, An Expository Dictionary of New Testament Words, vol. 3, 129.
[35] Vine, vol. 2, 18.
[36] Vine, vol. 4, 32.

keep from missing the spiritual "mark" of God's expectations must be sure that whatever activities he becomes involved in can be performed in faith. The thought continues into chapter fifteen, covering the first three verses. The ninth principle in this section is that believers ought to follow the example of Christ, seeking the benefit of others, rather than pleasing themselves.

This study is typical of the way that Bible principles should be gleaned, in order that the will of God be put into action for life circumstances that are not specified in Scripture. Obviously, a diligent search of the Scriptures is necessary to assure that one is not violating any of the revealed commandments or principles of God's Word in the conduct of his life.

Since the Bible is an objective source of information concerning God's will, there is not much debate among Bible believers concerning the existence of the moral will of God. At that point, however, there is a division about whether or not the non-determinative will of God also includes a specific plan that is tailor-made for the individual. Those traditionalists who admit to such a specific plan attempt to follow indicators that they believe are from God. Guidance from God is often seen in circumstances, "open doors," and inner impressions. This approach has been attacked as unduly subjective, but in reality, both systems of decision making require a measure of reliance upon subjective information.

Subjectivity

Inconsistency of opposition. It has been objected that a system of seeking the individual will of God must be subjective.[37] This subject will be dealt with further in chapter five, as the internalization of the will of God is studied. However, the objection may be answered partially by saying that the traditional system of discerning the will of God goes through all of the objective steps recommended by Friesen. It then relies upon indicators that are believed to come from God, rather than the subjective "wisdom" he recommends. Friesen discounts the interpretation of circumstances, "open doors," etc., in the discernment of God's will.[38] In actuality, his view relies heavily upon the evaluation of those things in his search for "wisdom." He simply does not attach any Divine significance to them! He admits as much in the following statement concerning the interpretation of circumstances:

> That does not mean that circumstances are unimportant to the wisdom view. Quite the contrary. Since circumstances provide the context in which a decision is made, they are a key source of wisdom for the

---

[37] Garry Friesen, Decision Making and the Will of God, 130.
[38] Ibid., 133-135.

decision maker. They must be evaluated, not to determine some clue from God, but to help decide the advisability of a given course of action.[39]

Hearts or heads? Friesen says that, "God does not reveal His individual will for our decisions through inner impressions upon our hearts."[40] However, he still seems to think that it is proper for believers to make decisions based upon inner impressions of their *heads!* Thus, even the practice of the gifts of the Holy Spirit is not governed by God's direction, but it simply becomes the decision of the individual believer:

> The gift of teaching, for example, can be a "full-time" teaching position or a weekly Bible study. The place that the gift is used could be with junior boys or college women, in Sunday School or one-on-one discipleship, in a local church or at a Bible school. These decisions are determined by spiritual expediency.[41]

While it is not denied that the gift can be used in all of the above ways, that does not mean that a given individual should simply rely upon human wisdom in choosing how to

---

[39] Ibid., 272.
[40] Ibid., 363.
[41] Ibid., 339.

use it. Only God knows best how, when, and where that gift should be used. He foresees factors that the Christian cannot see. Whatever Friesen means by "spiritual expediency," it seems inferior to reliance upon the foreknowledge of God, for only He has the right to determine how His laborers should function in His vineyard.

Further inconsistencies. The inconsistency of Friesen's thought seems evident when his reaction to subjectivity is compared with his attempt to discard the principle of tithing to the local church today:

> Under grace, the tithe has been replaced by the principle of proportionate giving. It is not difficult to compute 10 percent of one's income; but how much is "as he may prosper?" It is neither a specific amount nor a particular percentage.[42]

At best, Friesen's plan is subjective.[43] Inconsistency in Friesen's view is again seen when he declares that the *method*

---

[42] Ibid., 368.

[43] Traditionalists admit that decisions can involve some subjectivity, and offerings beyond the tithe fit into this category. As for the tithe, the moral will of God may be more definitive than Friesen thinks. The use of the participial form of θησαυριζω in I Corinthians 16:2 should be

used by God in calling Saul and Barnabas (Acts 13) is not normative, but the *principles* Friesen finds there are! Arbitrarily he says, "We should not look or listen for some dramatic call; but we should emulate the wisdom displayed by the Holy Spirit. . . ."[44] Since man cannot reason on the same level as God can, a wise man should ask God for direction, rather than lean to his own understanding (Proverbs 3:5-6).

A further proof of inconsistency is seen in Friesen's views on Genesis 24. After denying that "God has selected a mate in his individual will for each person,"[45] he says that if Rebekah's family had failed to cooperate, Abraham's servant would ". . . look to other families for the woman of God's

---

compared to the Septuagint's usage of the similar noun, θησαυρος, in Malachi 3:10. This could well lead to the conclusion that the principle of storehouse tithing in the Old Testament is carried over into the New Testament dispensation, with the local church becoming the place of the "storehouse." It is surprising that Friesen, who finds subjectivity so loathsome, would overlook this objective direction for giving.
[44] Friesen, 324.
[45] Ibid., 300.

choice."[46] One cannot help but wonder how, in Friesen's view, there could even *be* a "woman of God's choice."[47]

Scriptural subjectivity. Total objectivity in decision making (where the Scripture is not definitive) is neither possible nor Scriptural. Romans 14:5 requires that ". . . every man be fully persuaded in his own mind" about things not specified in Scripture. The "persuasion" idea is πληροφορεισθω, the present imperative passive form of the root, πληροθορεω, which means, "a full assurance, entire confidence."[48] Interestingly, this persuasion takes place in the believer's "mind" (dative of νους, signifying the "seat of reflective consciousness, comprising the faculties of perception and understanding, those of feeling, judging, and determining").[49] In this context, νους can even mean "opinion,"[50] since the chapter deals with things about which individual believers may disagree with one another. Thus, there

---

[46] Ibid.
[47] Friesen says (pages 151-152): "Any decision made within the moral will of God is acceptable to God." Perhaps he could more consistently refer to a "*category* of women of God's choice," rather than to a "*woman* of God's choice."
[48] Vine, vol. 1, 84.
[49] Ibid., vol. 3, 69.
[50] BAG, 4th rev. ed., s.v "νους," 547..

is to be a certain Scriptural subjectivity, with individuals properly coming to varying firm conclusions without being judgmental toward each other (verse 3).

Seeking the peace that God gives is no more subjective than relying upon human wisdom to make a decision. After the objective study of God's Word is completed, both the traditional "peace" method and Friesen's "wisdom" method rely upon subjective considerations for final decision making.[51] The problem, then, seems to be that Friesen wants to use the information available to the traditionalist in making decisions, but refuses to credit God with being responsible for leading the believer to that information.

<u>Summary</u>

There are two aspects of the will of God that are immediately apparent in the Scriptures. There is the sovereign, or determinative, will (about which man has no choice), and the general, or moral will, which is revealed in the Bible. The determinative will is that which God causes to take place,

---

[51] Friesen's "wisdom sources for marriage" are the Bible, spiritual counselors, common sense, and personal desires (pages 304-306). The latter two are subjective. In practice, Friesen's view is not much different from that of traditionalists, when it comes to subjectivity.

which is not necessarily revealed to man in advance. From man's viewpoint, it can only be discerned after the fact. That principle is especially true in relation to man's salvation, since man usually makes his decision to accept Christ without being aware of God's election. In order to give man the privilege of making decisions, God had to limit Himself and the expression of His sovereignty. God's Self-limitation provides a logical basis for human accountability in the making of decisions.

The non-determinative will of God includes that aspect which is called the general, or moral, will. It is found in the Bible and places a binding obligation upon all men. Where the Bible has spoken, man has only one legitimate decision, which is to agree with God. First, man must take note of the direct commandments of God's Word in light of dispensational and cultural factors. Then, Bible principles must be taken into account and applied to life situations. Failure to obey Bible commandments and follow Bible principles is sin.

The debate among believers of God's Word concerns the making of decisions that are not dictated by Bible commandments or principles. There is a measure of subjectivity that enters into decision making, regardless of which of the two positions one may claim. The "peace" method admits to relying upon inward impressions, interpreting them as partial guidance from God. Those of the "wisdom" school consider their position to be objective, but such a claim is not truly founded on fact. The truth is, that after the objective facts of the Bible are considered, there are still subjective factors that enter into the making of many decisions.

Chapter 3

The Specific Will of God in the Old Testament

The Controversy

This chapter will attempt to demonstrate that there is an individual will of God for each believer, according to the Old Testament. Coder says that God's will is wonderfully detailed (Psalm 37:23), continuous (Isaiah 58:11), and specific (Isaiah 30:21).[52] Each of these passages will be exegeted in this chapter, along with others. Two traditionalists describe the will of God in these ways:

> There is a divine blueprint for each one of God's people. It is exactly suited to our own peculiar needs, so that it enables us to make the most of our possibilities. It has not only this life in view, but also the life to come. It is easy to discover what it is. In fact, the Lord is more desirous that we learn His plan than we ourselves are. He has made every provision to enable us to follow it.[53]

---

[52] S. Maxwell Coder, God's Will for Your Life, 12-13.
[53] Ibid., 7-8.

God has a specific will which differs with each individual Christian. . . . God has a tailor-made plan for the life of every believer. The details, of course, are not spelled out in the Scriptures.[54]

The above-stated position seems preferable to the view of Friesen, who asserts: "The idea that God has an ideal individual will for each believer which must be discovered in order to make right decisions has been abandoned."[55] Since it is clearly impossible for both views to be right, it is necessary that the Scripture be studied carefully in this regard. It will ultimately be seen that both Testaments speak of an individual will of God, but first the testimony of the Old Testament will be considered.

Old Testament Proofs

The Old Testament deals often with the issue of individual guidance. This is disputed by Friesen, who denies the fact of individual guidance. He acknowledges that the ". . . Old Testament is replete with accounts of men and women who received direct guidance leading them to take on a certain

---

[54] J. Herbert Kane, <u>Understanding Christian Missions</u>, 43.
[55] Friesen, 428.

vocation . . . or do a certain thing."[56] He also cites many examples of it in the New Testament,[57] but questions whether such examples are normative (binding upon every believer). His objections to these examples being normative hinge upon the following points: (1) there is an insufficient number of recorded examples, (2) most of the examples are of individuals who occupied special places in God's program, (3) the examples deal with only a few decisions, and (4) the method of communication was supernatural.[58]

In the same order as his charges, it can be fairly answered that: (1) there are no clear examples of individuals making right decisions in which the Bible says they had no inner leading, (2) history normally focuses upon special people, but in order for others to be omitted, Friesen would have to say "all," rather than "most," (3) the relative importance of decisions makes some more historically noteworthy than others, and (4) it is simply not provable that all cases involved supernatural revelation.[59]

---

[56] Ibid., 89.
[57] Ibid., 89-90.
[58] Ibid., 90-91.
[59] See the discussion of Acts 15:25-28 and Acts 16:6-7 in chapter five of this book.

<u>Dispensationalism</u>. It is unfair to discount all examples on the basis that they took place during revelatory days, making each situation an exception, rather than the rule. Of course, the entire Bible had not yet been written when the events of the Old Testament were occurring, but it is a violation of Scripture to eliminate all such teachings merely on that basis. Some principles, such as holiness, obedience, the sanctity of marriage, and personal faith in the shed blood of a substitute (to name just a few), transcend the dispensations. The mere fact that one reads of these events occurring before or during the days of special revelation does not mean that they have no relevancy once the canon was closed. The theological "baby" must not be thrown out with the dispensational "bathwater."

<u>Biblical theology</u>. Friesen's view has some interesting implications when viewed from the standpoint of Biblical theology, or the recognition of progressive revelation. He states boldly that his "wisdom view" conquers subjectivity:

> Christian decision making is grounded on the objective truth of God's *moral* will. According to the Bible, the only aspect of God's will that must be known, the only aspect that can be known, is God's *moral* will. And 100

percent of God's moral will—not 80 percent, not 90 percent, but 100 percent—has been revealed in the Bible (emphasis his).[60]

While the strength of Friesen's conviction is apparent, some questions should be asked concerning how much of the moral will of God existed before and during the time of the writing of the Bible. There were approximately twenty-five centuries of human history before man received the Ten Commandments. Even then, there was only one copy available; hence, the "Bible" was hardly a household item. Was it allowable for the Jews to violate any or all of those commandments up until the time they were inscripturated? It certainly does not seem so from the account of Cain, who was held accountable for murder, despite having no Bible, nor does the Bible record any statement God made to Cain forbidding such an act. Were not Gentiles under any moral law until they became proselyte Jews, or until the New Testament local church included them? If "100 percent" of God's moral law has been revealed in the Bible, then those who lived before there was any Bible could not have been justly held accountable for their sins.

---

[60] Friesen, 264-265.

Since there is no Biblical record of God's instructions to Cain and Abel, was it simply an accident that Abel offered an acceptable sacrifice, while poor Cain's was unacceptable? Why would God punish Noah's contemporaries, or the inhabitants of Sodom and Gomorrah, if His moral will was incomplete?

Is it not the argument of Romans 1:18-28 that, both before and after much of Scripture had been written, God still dealt with man both internally and externally? Is it a proper use of "special revelation" to apply it to Abraham's servant's experience in Genesis 24, or should that term be reserved for Moses' inscripturation of the event centuries later? Where is it proven that every time God revealed Himself to man it involved some miraculous external means, as opposed to internal leading? When God "spoke" to man, was it always done audibly? It is contended here that all of the above Scriptural circumstances required some type of internal message from God in the revelation of His will.

It seems that any system that holds man accountable to nothing but the Bible cannot fairly expect much from those individuals who lived prior to its writing. In fact, the entire dispensations of Conscience and Human Government would seem to have little basis in the non-determinative will of God, if Friesen's view is accepted. Surely the moral will of God would have to be redefined, if God has never communicated His will in any other form than through the written Word or "special revelation to special people."

Arbitrariness. It may be answered that the requirements of God for individuals throughout history provide a cumulative statement of the moral will of God for man, as the science of Biblical theology teaches. If so, there seems to be an arbitrariness in the assumption that all of the *requirements* were normative, but the ways in which they were revealed are not allowed to continue. These problems should be dealt with, in connection with the "wisdom" view of the will of God. With these preliminary thoughts in mind, the student of the Old Testament can find credibility in those passages that speak of individual guidance.

Psalm 143:10.

The Old Testament uses sixteen different Hebrew words to describe "will," referring to both God and man.[61] One of these words is רעון, used over fifty times in the Old Testament.[62] Addressing God in Psalm 143:10, David adds the second person, masculine suffix, ("thy will") to refer to God's "desire" or "pleasure."[63] The phrase to be considered here implores, "Teach me to do thy will. . . ."

---

[61] James Strong, The Exhaustive Concordance of the Bible, 1160-1173.

[62] TWOT, s. v. "רעון," by William White, vol. 2, 859.

[63] Ibid.

The context. The request for teaching fits into a context which includes two divisions of the chapter. The first six verses indicate that David faced great opposition at the hand of his enemies, so he sought God's help. He felt that he qualified for this help, because he maintained a spiritual "thirst" (verse 6). The word *Selah* divides this portion from the latter six verses, which express David's desire to know God and His ways better. He asked God to deliver him from his enemies (verse 9), and to give instruction about God's will (verses 8-9).[64]

Teaching and leading. David wanted to be taught what God desired. The request to "teach" is the imperative form of למד, which denotes both education and training, and is related to the common word for "oxgoad."[65] He followed the poetic parallelism of the couplet by requesting that God "lead" (imperative of נחה) him in this matter.[66] נחה ". . . is sometimes synonymous with *nahag* 'to herd' to a predetermined destination."[67] The "land of uprightness" to which David wanted to be led was not Canaan, since he was already living there. It is evidently a figure of speech for a basically trouble-free lifestyle.[68] Since David requested both

---

[64] W. Graham Scroggie, The Psalms, 87-90.

[65] TWOT, s. v. "למד," by Walter C. Kaiser, vol. 1, 480.

[66] It is this parallelism that seems to speak against the likelihood of David simply wanting to know how to do that which he already knew he should do. "Teach" seems parallel to "lead."

[67] TWOT, s. v. "נחה," vol. 2, 568.

[68] Charles Haddon Spurgeon, The Treasury of David, vol. 7, 324-325.

teaching and leading, this is not the determinative will of God, nor is it the general will of God. He was asking God to direct him internally to the spiritual destination at which God wanted him to arrive. The "oxgoad" comparison indicates that God also uses external means in training men to do His will. David knew that it would be better to feel the temporary pain of the goad than to fail to do the will of God.

Application. It can be learned from this portion then, that the spiritual believer has a desire to know and do God's will, and that it is proper for him to pray for specific guidance from God. He then can expect God to work in his life, both internally (what some might call "subjectively") and externally, in the revelation of that will.

Psalm 32:8

Answer to prayer. There are numerous other prayers for guidance recorded in the Psalms (5:8; 19:12-14; 25:4-5, 21; 27:11; 31:3-4; 86:11; 119:5, 12, 35-36, 80, 133, 176; and 141:3-4).[69] God promises to answer these prayers in Psalm 32:8. To do so, He pledges, "I will instruct thee and teach thee in the way which thou shalt go: I will guide thee with mine eye." Of this verse, Coder says, "An individual pathway is in view, as distinguished from the

---

[69] M. Blaine Smith, Knowing God's Will, 59.

general way of righteousness set before all Christians."[70] The following study will attempt to prove that statement.

Spiritual prerequisites. In this verse, the revelation of God's perfect plan is promised after the individual believer has established proper fellowship with God. David had struggled with unconfessed sin, causing severe physical and emotional problems for him (verses 3-4). He came to the point of confession and found forgiveness (verse 5). This established a relationship in which he could claim God's promise of personal instruction. When God replies[71] in verses 8-9, He makes three promises and encourages David to avoid stubbornly living without understanding.[72]

---

[70] Coder, 11.

[71] Friesen (page 100) supposes that David might be the speaker here, fulfilling his promise to teach sinners in Psalm 51:13. This seems highly unlikely, since David is clearly addressing God in 32:4-7. The "thee" of verse 6 is One to whom prayers are made, so He is not in need of teaching. There is an obvious change at the end of verse 7, indicated by *Selah*. However, the "thee" of verse 8 appears to be included in the "righteous" of verse 11. David promised in Psalm 51:13 to teach "transgressors." It seems more likely that the speaker is David in the first seven verses, then God responds in 8-11. Further evidence that God is personally speaking to David in verse 8 is found in the usage of singular suffixes with the promises, whereas a general message to "transgressors" would be expected to appear in the plural.

[72] Scroggie,188.

Three promises. The first promise is אַשְׂכִּילְךָ, which is Hiphil imperfect, first person singular, with a second person masculine singular suffix. This signifies that which God will do for a single individual. The root, שׂכל, means "to make prudent" in this verse.[73] "Teach" is the same form, from ירה, meaning "to throw, or cast." It denotes a strong sense of control by the subject (God).[74] "Guide (from יעץ) with mine eye" means "counsel with an eye upon you."[75]

Application. The application of this verse is that God controls man by teaching him. This teaching is personal, rather than generic, and comes after man finds forgiveness and spiritual refuge in God. Thus, it again is apparent that God works on man internally and individually, desiring to control man's lifestyle by controlling his reasoning and understanding. God further pledges to give counsel with a watchful "eye" upon man.

Proverbs 3:5-6

Spiritual commitment. A favorite passage of many people is Proverbs 3:5-6: "Trust in the Lord with all thine heart; and lean not unto thine own understanding. In all thy ways acknowledge him, and he shall direct thy paths."

---

[73] Samuel Prideaux Tregelles, ed., Gesenius' Hebrew and Chaldee Lexicon, 790.

[74] TWOT, s.v "ירה," by John E. Hartley, vol. 1, 403.

[75] Ibid., s. v. "יעץ," 391.

The essence of this portion is that every believer is commanded to trust God with the totality of his immaterial nature, and to acknowledge God in every aspect of life. He has the promise that God will give clear direction in return. The proverb speaks of obedience to God's Word (verse 1), which is a consistent prerequisite to special guidance from God. However, this is not merely a directive to read the Bible, but entails much more, both in commitment and benefits. The verses to be studied here are surrounded by promises of blessing, which result from following God, rather than leaning upon one's own wisdom. Such blessings include longevity (verse 2), spiritual and social favor (verse 4), health (verse 8), and prosperity (verse 10).

Total trust. The command to "trust" is בטח, whose root ". . . expresses that sense of well-being and security which results from having something or someone in whom to place confidence."[76] The idea is to find security in trusting God, because confidence in Him has a superior validity when compared to any other kind of dependence.[77] "Thine heart" (לב) refers to the totality of man's inner being. The word is

---

[76] Ibid., s.v. "בטח," by John N. Oswalt, 101.
[77] Ibid.

46

used variously to mean "heart," in the sense of one's emotions, affections, thoughts, will, purpose, and intellect.[78]

In this context the unqualified "all" is used, so it is fair to conclude that every aspect of man's immaterial nature is here intended. Furthermore, contrary to those who say that Christians are left to make decisions without ". . . an infinite God guiding finite human beings,"[79] believers are specifically instructed not to "lean" (שען = "an attitude of trust"[80]) to their own understanding. It appears, then, that making decisions based upon available human wisdom, without seeking direction from God, constitutes sinful attitudes and actions.[81]

Complete acknowledgement. The acknowledgement of God is to be done in all of man's "ways," without exception, in order for individuals to qualify for special direction from God.[82] "Ways," in verse 6, is a form of דרך. This word signifies

---

[78] Tregelles, 427.
[79] Yancey, 25.
[80] TWOT, s.v. "שען," by Hermann J. Austel, 945.
[81] Later, this will be qualified to include only those decisions that have foreseeable lasting consequences.
[82] This is special direction, not merely general direction from the Bible. The Bible always gives the same instruction, whether man acknowledges God or not. This is direction for which man must qualify, by fully acknowledging God.

a path worn by constant walking, and is metaphorical for the actions and behavior of men.[83] In all of his "ways," man is to "acknowledge" (דעהו) God. This is a Kal imperative from ידע, which means, "to know, to perceive, to discover, to become acquainted."[84] Thus, in all of man's ways he can gain knowledge about God. The moral will of God is found in the Bible, but this speaks of another source of knowledge about God, which seems to refer to the individual will. The promise to the man who habitually acknowledges God in his behavior is that God will direct (ישר = "straighten")[85] his "path" (ארה = "lifestyle").[86]

Individual will. There are good reasons to apply this "straightening of the lifestyle" to the individual will of God. The fact that it speaks of what God will do in the *future*, and that He will do it in response to certain actions of men, is weighty. The sovereign will of God can be ruled out immediately, because it is not conditioned by man's responses to God. It will come to pass, regardless of whether man obeys or not. This cannot be a promise to the Old Testament saints

---

[83] TWOT, s. v. "דרך," by Herbert Wolf, vol. 1, 197–198.
[84] Tregelles, 333.
[85] Ibid., 375.
[86] TWOT, s. v. "ארה," by Victor P. Hamilton, vol.1, 71.

that God will provide more of His moral will, because the writing of the Bible was not accomplished conditionally as a reward for obedience. An in-depth study of יָשַׁר ("to straighten") will further demonstrate its applicability to a precise, specific will.

Preciseness. Friesen equates this word with "making successful," in order to allow for a general (moral) will of God to be seen in Proverbs 3:6.[87] However, he appears to go beyond the Scriptural usage of the word, in order to support a preconceived application. The Hebrew root is used in three distinct ways: (1) literally, "to make straight," (2) ethically, "to make upright," and (3) idiomatically, signifying approval, when used with the "eyes (of a person)."[88] The third possibility can be eliminated because of the absence of the word for "eyes" in Proverbs 3:6.

Since the passage speaks of a lifestyle, rather than of material substance, the figurative (ethical) usage fits best here. The figurative application is based, however, upon a proper understanding of the literal meaning. When the word is used literally (dealing in the physical realm), it appears to signify

---

[87] Friesen, 98.
[88] TWOT, s. v. "יָשַׁר," by Donald J. Wiseman, vol. 1, 417.

specific, precise direction. It is used of carrying the Ark of the Covenant, traveling so precisely that they ". . . turned not aside to the right hand or to the left (I Samuel 6:12)." It speaks of water flowing ". . . straight down to the west side (II Chronicles 32:30)." Ezekiel's vision of the four wheels included wings that pointed "straight" toward each other (Ezekiel 1:23). Finally, Elihu used the term to describe the way that "directs" the lightning in a rainstorm (Job 37:3). While man views lightning as striking at random, God evidently has its precise path planned intricately.

With a proper understanding of the usage of ישר in the literal, physical realm, the student can proceed to apply it to ethical circumstances. In Proverbs 4:25, King Solomon figuratively speaks of spiritual values when he commands man's eyes to look "straight" ahead. Isaiah 40:3 instructs the Messiah's forerunner to make a "straight" highway for Him. Regardless of whatever eschatological implications may be found in Isaiah 15:1-13, God had a message for the historical Cyrus wherein God promised to "direct" *all* of man's ways. This statement, using the plural, can certainly point to detailed, specific direction, rather than just a general lifestyle. This same spiritual precision is also obviously pictured in the need for man to walk a "straight" way (Psalm 5:8; Jeremiah 31:9), and in the way that the Godly man is to be "directed" by righteousness (Proverbs 11:5). This seems to be the most accurate understanding of the word when it is found in Proverbs 3:6. Only the specific, individual will of God seems to fit this term.

Application. To summarize Proverbs 3:5-6, the following principles can be discerned: (1) trusting God gives superior security, (2) trusting God is an internal experience, (3) man should mistrust his own understanding of things, (4) all of men's actions and behavioral habits should be seen as resources for learning more about God, (5) God wants to internally direct man's lifestyle, and (6) God's direction gives man a straight, precise path.

Psalm 37:23

The context. As in other dispensations, there was a relationship between man's trust and God's blessing under the Law, according to Psalm 37:3-6. The conditional promises given there set the table for the statement in verse 23 that, "the steps of a good man are ordered by the Lord." It seems reasonable to conclude that God's blessing, as a result of man's trust, extends to the ordering of man's steps. In other words, the man who trusts God also receives direction from God. The psalm deals with many contrasts between the wicked and the righteous, as is seen by the comparisons in verse 2-3, 10-11, 16, 17, 18-20, 21, 22, 28, 29-36, and 37-39.

Individual steps. As part of the pattern of contrasts, the believer described as "good" is said to receive special directions.

This seems to be an obvious addition to general revelation, which is available even to the wicked. The "steps" of verse 23, whose root is מִצְעָד, refer to a pattern for living.[89] When seen in the light of the promise of blessing (especially in verses 4-5), this appears to be more than just general revelation given to all.[90] It is specific guidance for a specific class.

Neither does this "ordering" speak of the sovereign will of God, because it specifically applies to a "good" man, indicating that he somehow qualifies for this privilege on the basis of his spiritual character. If the sovereign will were in view, what would this verse be saying about the wicked man? Would he not be under the sovereign control of God?

Neither the moral will nor the sovereign will are acceptably in view here, if the "ordering" is something from which the wicked are excluded. It is said that these steps are "ordered" by the Lord. That significant word is from כוּן, which, in the Polal as it is here, signifies, "to be established."[91]

---

[89] TWOT, s. v. "צעד," by John E. Hartley, vol. 2, 771-772.
[90] The desires of the heart will differ from individual to individual, and God's promise to bring them to pass has a specific flavor.
[91] Benjamin Davidson, The Analytical Hebrew and Chaldee Lexicon, 373-374.

The conclusion is that the believer is happy following God's plan, because his delight is in God's דֶּרֶךְ.[92] This portion should be seen as yet further evidence that God has a specific plan for every individual, which brings happiness and security to all who will follow Him. This ordering of steps is not available to the wicked, but it is accomplished as an internal ministry to the believer.

Isaiah 30:21

The same pattern. Although it has an eschatological application, some writers have concluded that Isaiah 30:21 is germane to the study of individual guidance.[93] God says to Israel, "And thine ears shall hear a word behind thee, saying, This is the way, walk ye in it, when ye turn to the right hand,

---

[92] NIV translates this, "The Lord delights in the way of the man. . . ." If this were a proper translation, it would seem to support Friesen's view. The assumption would be that man chooses his own way, then God approves of man's choice. However, it appears that this translation wrongly identifies the antecedents of the two masculine pronouns. It would be unusual for God to delight in man's way, when God's ways are "higher" than man's ways (Isaiah 55:8-9). Also, if God is the One ordering the steps, then the "way" being traveled is not originally man's way, but God's. By contrast, it would make sense if the verse speaks of man delighting in God's way as man moves "upward" in his lifestyle, seeing the superiority of God's way.

[93] Coder, 12-13.

and when ye turn to the left." Chapter thirty of Isaiah's prophecy speaks of direction from God, coming through Millennial "teachers," (verse 20).

At first glance, this seems to vary from the usual pattern of an individual getting his heart right with God before receiving direction. The hearers are called "rebellious children" in verse 1, and there are numerous indictments of Israel's ungodly living in the chapter (verses 1-2, 9-11, 12, 15-16). In actuality, the pattern is intact in this passage. The immediate preceding context reveals that Israel will be chastened by the Lord for her sin (verses 16-18), and that she will repent and "cry" unto God (verse 19). God's relations with His people change in the following context to include blessing that stems from obedience. In fact, "The genuineness of Israel's conversion is indicated in verse 22, what they had honored and loved, they now loathe. . . ."[94]

Teachers from God. The "teachers," from whom the word of direction is given, are indicated by a plural participial noun from מורה, which has been previously cited as indicating both education and training. In this passage, it probably refers

---

[94] F. C. Jennings, Studies in Isaiah, 367.

to the lessons taught through adversity, as indicated by verse 20.[95]

    <u>Message from God</u>. The message to be heard in verse 21 is of the "way" God wants His people to walk, and again the "way" is the frequently-used דרך, indicating a lifestyle. While all of this is consistent with the pattern already discerned for the specific leading of God, this passage may be disputed as an example. There seems to be contextual reasons to conclude that God is not dealing with *individual*, but rather with *national*, guidance in this text. Nevertheless, there is a surprising use of singular suffixes to the noun ("thine ears" = אזניך)[96] and pronoun ("behind thee" = מאחריך).[97] The "word" and the "ears" are not to be taken literally, because the "teachers" are adversity and affliction, indicating that God teaches man through circumstances.

    Although this is a Millennial portion, it does not disagree with what this chapter has seen of the Dispensation of Law, nor does it disagree with what will be seen in the next chapter regarding the age of the Local Church. That is to be

---

[95] Ibid.
[96] Ibid., 16.
[97] Ibid., 461.

expected, since principles of guidance seem to transcend the dispensations. In fairness, this should not be seen as conclusively teaching the individual will of God, due to its likely application to the nation of Israel, rather than to individuals, but the passage certainly does not threaten the traditional view of guidance in any way.

<u>Isaiah 58:11</u>

There is a promise of continual guidance in Isaiah 58:11. This is another passage with Millennial overtones, teaching that ". . . the Lord shall guide thee continually."

<u>Message for individuals</u>. God uses the plural "they" in verse 2 as He speaks of the nation, continuing with the plural terms through verse 6. Then He makes individual application by switching to the singular usages in verse 7, following that with a series of singular verb forms. Thus, the promise of verse 11 is that the Lord ". . . shall guide thee . . . ," containing the second person *singular* suffix (ונחך)[98]

<u>Continual leading</u>. The root word, נחה, means, "to govern," or "to lead," as of troops into battle.[99] It ". . . represents

---

[98] Ibid., 543.
[99] Tregelles, 542.

the conducting of one along the right path."[100] This conducting is to take place "continually" (תמיד = "perpetually").[101]

The results of renewal. Once again, the promise of guidance follows a time of spiritual renewal. This is evidenced by the heart change which takes place between the false motives described in verse 3 and the proper motives of verse 6. Verse 8 speaks of a glorious blessing from God, and verse 9 promises answered prayer. It is abundantly consistent in Scripture that God's special guidance to individuals comes after their hearts are restored to fellowship with God, and after they begin to practice obedience to Him.

Proverbs 16:9

Yet another passage that deals with guidance is Proverbs 16:9. There it is stated that, even though man makes his own plans, ". . . the Lord directeth his steps." While it is sometimes difficult to build a strong contextual case in the Proverbs, there are indications in the preceding context of spiritual preparations that should be made in man's heart. Verse 3 speaks of a special commitment to the Lord, and verse 6

---

[100] TWOT, s. v. "נחה," by Leonard J. Coppes, vol. 2, 568.
[101] Tregelles, 86.

explains that men depart from evil by fearing Him. Verse 7 speaks of a special benefit that comes when man pleases God, and righteousness is extolled as being superior to material wealth, in verse 8. Thus, even in this passage it can be seen that there are spiritual prerequisites for the guidance that believers may receive from God.

Man's way. The first part of verse 9 gives attention to the believer's own scheme of things. It is said that a man's "heart deviseth" his דֶּרֶךְ. The word for "heart" is לֵב, seen to refer to the ". . . totality of man's inner or immaterial nature."[102] Thus, God asserts that man relies upon internal direction in decision making. "Deviseth" is יְחַשֵּׁב, which is Piel imperfect. The root is חָשַׁב, which in the Piel means "think, meditate, consider."[103] Hence, it is within man's innermost being that he meditates upon the lifestyle that he plans to lead. This planning is contrasted to God's intervention, as described in the second half of the couplet.

God's way. The second half of the verse is introduced by a ו consecutive, which indicates an action following that which has already been mentioned. That is, man "devises," *then*

---

[102] TWOT, s. v. "לֵב," by Andrew Bowling, vol. 1, 466.
[103] Tregelles, 311.

the Lord "directs." The verb is a Hiphil imperfect, from כוּן. This Hiphil root can mean, "to direct, to aim, as a weapon."[104] It is thus seen as a term indicating precise, rather than general, direction. The following explanation is helpful in this study:

> The sense of well-being which results from being under God's hand. . . . If our heart is fixed on God (Ps 112:7, *etc.*) then we may be sure that he will establish (also direct, order) our ways (Ps 37:23; 90:17; Prov 16:9). Apart from this kind of confidence, a person's ways are temporary and shaky. But with it there comes a certainty, a rightness . . . which imparts some of the glory of the infinite to the finite.[105]

This proverb says that God works internally with the believer, to give him a sense of fixity and assurance which results from God's "aiming" him in the right direction.

Man's steps. The "steps" that are "aimed" by God are from צַעַד, the methodical walking of a path.[106] Thus, it is

---

[104] Ibid., 387.
[105] TWOT, s. v. "כוּן," by John S. Oswalt, vol. 1, 433-434.
[106] Tregelles, 714.

man's entire direction in life that God overrules in providing individual guidance.[107]

Application. Several ideas pertinent to this study are confirmed in Proverbs 16:9. First, God again condemns man's practice of depending upon his own wisdom in the making of decisions. Second, when man makes his own decisions, he basically does so from subjective reasoning. Third, God intervenes in the believer's thought processes to "aim" him in the right direction. Fourth, God obviously cares about the specific details of man's decisions. Fifth, God wants to direct the methodical "walking" of life's path by His children.

Further Old Testament Proofs

The above observations from Old Testament passages are fortified by these statements from Psalm 25:

> Shew me thy ways, O Lord; teach me thy paths. Lead me in thy truth, and teach me. . . . Good and upright is the Lord; therefore will he teach sinners in the way.

---

[107] God speaks against the folly of man depending upon his own wisdom and might in Jeremiah 10:23, and the superiority of God's thought processes is clearly stated in Isaiah 55:8-9. For further evidence that God affects man's thoughts, see Proverbs 21:1.

The meek will he guide in judgment: and the meek will he teach his way. . . . What man is he that feareth the Lord? Him shall he teach in the way that he shall choose (verses 4-5, 8-9, 12).

The sinfulness and folly of man's reliance upon his own "wisdom" (Proverbs 3:5) is because he is *incapable* of properly directing his own steps. In the words of Jeremiah 10:23,". . . the way of man is not in himself: it is not in man that walketh to direct his steps." It is far better to depend upon God's "directing" than upon man's "devising."

<u>Summary</u>

Chapter five will look in detail at the illustration of special guidance found in Genesis 24. Further attention will be given to that Old Testament passage later, but the principles thus far gleaned can now be summarized.

In each portion of Scripture studied, it is evident that there are spiritual prerequisites for individual guidance. This guidance is not easily accessible to every believer, because it requires the believer to demonstrate a measure of spiritual maturity. Second, God works both externally and internally to direct man into His will. Several passages have been cited here that emphasize the internal aspect of that leading. Third, God's plan is detailed and specific, describing a lifestyle in which the particulars are already planned by the omniscient God. Next, the knowledge of the existence of that plan gives security to the believer who follows. Because God's "eye" is upon His child, the one who follows His plan has assurance that it is right. Fifth, it is wrong for the individual to make his own plans, apart from consulting God. Sixth, though man is always tempted to follow the dictates of his own inner thought processes, God desires to aim him in the right direction. This involves God affecting man's thoughts to give man access to a higher level of thought potential (see Isaiah 55:8-9).

It seems almost absurd that one could read the Old Testament and conclude that God does not have a knowable, specific plan for individual believers in Christ. It is the uniform testimony of David, Solomon, Isaiah, and Jeremiah, that God has a detailed plan for individuals. These writers also agree that God works within man to influence man to think His thoughts. Thus, it is a mystery that committed Bible students could deny the existence of an individualized plan of God for believers.

Chapter 4

The Specific Will of God in the New Testament

The Old Testament is not unique in teaching a specific, individual will of God. In fact, the New Testament has perhaps even more instructions to be considered. An exegetical consideration of several key New Testament passages will reveal three truths: (1) God has spiritual prerequisites for revealing His individual will to believers, (2) He reveals it through both internal and external means, and (3) the end result is assurance for the Christian. As one writer states it, the New Testament gives testimony that:

> . . . Jesus explicitly speaks of taking the sort of responsibility for his followers that a shepherd takes for his sheep. And this responsibility clearly involves guidance. . . . God's guidance is not something reserved only for the Christian "heroes" but a precious gift given to each and every believer.[108]

Howard remarks that the Bible contains a complete, but not a comprehensive, revelation of the will of God. It is said to be complete, in the sense that every *area* of life is considered;

---

[108] M. Blaine Smith, 31, 33.

but it is not comprehensive, since not every *detail* of the individual's life is revealed.[109]

An opposing view is presented by Friesen. He says that in the first thirty years of church history (recorded in the book of Acts), there were no more than "... fifteen to twenty instances of direct, personal guidance. . . ," and that most of the time Paul merely evaluated circumstances to make decisions. [110] It is noteworthy, however, that the same author cites only *five* passages that describe Paul's decision process. If he thinks that fifteen to twenty recorded cases are insufficient for a normative pattern to develop, why does he conclude that the five he chooses are sufficient? Of course, the five passages cited do *not* say that Paul failed to pray for guidance, so they in no way argue against the traditional view.

Friesen says that guidance in the book of Acts came only through supernatural revelation, such as visions, angelic messengers, physical miracles, audible voices from God, or a prophet who had direct revelation. He concludes with the following: "Are there other recorded examples where detailed

---

[109] J. Grant Howard, Knowing God's Will and Doing It!, 30.
[110] Friesen, 90.

guidance was given through some means other than supernatural revelation? No.[111]

The fallacy of this statement can be seen by considering that Acts 15:25-28 says the Jerusalem church (". . . it seemed good unto us. . . . ") and the Holy Spirit (". . . it seemed good to the Holy Ghost. . . . ") agreed upon a matter of doctrinal application. This demonstrates that the Holy Spirit led the church in voting, as another means of revealing God's will, and that the church had an awareness of the Holy Spirit's approval. Also, in Acts 16:6-7, the Holy Spirit directed the location of Paul's ministry, in opposition to Paul's own prior decision making. In this passage, it would have been in agreement with the moral will of God for Paul to preach in Asia and Bithynia, but the Holy Spirit forbade him to go there. Apparently, God *did* care about the specifics of Paul's location and gave him individual direction that was different, no doubt, from the direction that He gave to others regarding Asia and Bithynia.

While the method of God's revelation of this information to Paul is not given in this text, it is clear that God's unwritten desires contradicted Paul's personal plans, and Paul somehow was made aware of it. This agrees with the

---

[111] Ibid., 91.

individual leading of God's Holy Spirit.[112] In fact, Romans 8:14 reveals that one of the evidences of salvation is the leading of the Holy Spirit. That statement is found in a context which deals with the Holy Spirit's internal ministry to the believer.

Although Friesen makes some erroneous statements in the attempt to support his hypothesis, he does have a commendable spirit with regard to the Word of God. In fact, he seems basically fair in his representation of the traditional view. He is worthy of appreciation for the following appraisal of his own conclusions:

> Although the examples do not prove an individual will of God, in fairness to the traditional view it must also

---

[112] Obviously, this is not conclusive. A case can be built for the assumption that this was the sovereign will of God, rather than the individual will. However, such a conclusion is not as simple as it may sound at the outset. Since the sovereign will can be known by man only after the fact, one must read into the story that Paul attempted to go, but was somehow forbidden by *external circumstances*. If Paul was forbidden by external circumstances, it would concur with the notion of an individual will to conclude that the circumstances could be pointers to help the individual know God's will. If this is the individual will, there are also internal ways that the Holy Spirit could have revealed it to Paul (lack of peace, for example). Thus, the individual will makes allowance for all of the possibilities, whereas the sovereign will theory limits God to dealing only externally.

be said that they do not disprove it either. The direct teaching of the Word of God must act as the final arbitrator.[113]

Since it is agreed that the direct teaching of the Word of God must be the final arbitrator, then there is great benefit in the exegesis of New Testament passages that give direct teaching concerning the will of God. Friesen's treatments limit themselves almost entirely to his understanding of the contexts of individual passages, with little or no grammatical work included.[114] While contextual work is a significant part of exegesis, it is not the entire process.[115] Furthermore, his

---

[113] Ibid., 93.

[114] For examples of this, see his chapter six, "Does Scripture Teach the 'Dot;'?"

[115] Friesen's analyses of contexts often result from a closed system of reasoning. He begins with the (proper) assumption that every commandment in the Bible is a part of the moral will of God. When he sees a commandment regarding the knowing or doing of God's will, he notes other commandments in its context, and concludes that the context is dealing only with the moral will of God, since commandments appear there. However, he fails to account for the fact that part of the moral will of God involves knowing and doing the individual will of God. In other words, no matter how clear the grammar of a verse may be, Friesen would not allow the possibility of a commandment concerning the individual will of God, since he sees all commandments as the moral

contextual work is arguable, because he fails to see possibilities in certain contexts that traditionalists can see.

A comparison of his statements on page 103 with those on pages 110-111 will reveal that he uses Colossians 1:9-10 to support his conclusions for Ephesians 5:17, while at the same time using Ephesians 5:17 to prove his view of Colossians 1:9. Such circular reasoning fails to prove its point. It can also be noted that he uses a number of support verses in each section, which might be impressive if they actually gave the support he assumes, but such is not necessarily the case.[116] The mere listing

---

will of God. He overlooks the intertwining of the two concepts in Scripture.

[116] He lists five particular passages in both sections, as if they indisputably prove his claims. Even a brief look at them reveals that there is room for debate in each passage. Of II Corinthians 5:9-10, why could not the apostle be speaking of labor and judgment that includes the individual will of God? Romans 8:14 says that every Christian has Holy Spirit leading, an idea which fully accords with the individual will. In Ephesians 5:10, discerning what is ". . . acceptable unto the Lord . . ." is a way to describe the specific will of God. Ephesians 6:6 speaks of internalizing the will of God, which again fits the individual idea. And in I John 3:22, the question should be asked whether ". . . keep his commandments . . ." is the equivalent of doing ". . . things that are pleasing . . . ," or if the apostle is encouraging a *combination* of obedient steps, coupled by the conjunction? It appears that *none* of these five

of references does not prove Friesen's point. When citing the Word of God to support a point in question, it is only fair if the cited passages actually provide real support. Friesen's use of references is as fallacious as his circular reasoning indicated earlier in this paragraph.

In the exegesis of New Testament passages, attention will be drawn first to passages that deal with *knowing* God's will, and then to those that speak of *doing* God's will.

Knowing God's Will

There is certainly a "knowable," specific will of God for every one of His children. The Apostle Paul desired to preach the Gospel in Asia and Bithynia, but God wanted him instead to go to Macedonia at that time (Acts 16:6-10). It would not have violated the *general* will of God for Paul to go to the other places, in light of the fact that Christians had been commissioned to go to all the world with the Gospel (Matthew 28:18-20). However, God's *specific* will was for Paul to go to Macedonia at that time, so He revealed His will to the apostle.

---

passages used in support of Friesen's conclusions for Colossians 1:9 and Ephesians 5:17 is immediately conclusive of his position.

One should not merely throw a dart at a map when selecting a field of service for God!

<u>Ephesians 5:17</u>

In Ephesians 5:17, Christians are commanded to be ". . . not unwise, but understanding what the will of the Lord is." Smith asserts that God makes a special effort to reveal His will to believers, in order that they may have adequate knowledge to obey Him fully.[117] The underlying assumption of Ephesians 5:17 is that this is the condition; thus, every believer has the responsibility to know what God expects of him.

The context. The preceding context gives a series of commandments which, if obeyed, demonstrates that the Christian has established a right relationship with God. This agrees with the Old Testament pattern of spiritual prerequisites for knowing the individual will of God. Briefly stated, the believer is to follow God (verse 1), avoid sin (verses 3-4), avoid evil associations (verses 5-11), and live with spiritual alertness and diligence (verses 14-16). Verse 10, in fact, reveals that the Godly walk involves a diligent effort of "testing" what is

---

[117] Smith, 10.

pleasing to the Lord,[118] and verse 14 speaks of Christ giving "light" to the obedient. Believers should neither be "fools" (lacking wisdom) in verse 15, nor "unwise" (lacking sense) in verse 17. The following context adds still other commandments and principles to the list, with verse 18 expanding the concept of mind control that was touched upon in verses 14-17.

Conquering ignorance. The command to avoid being "unwise" is μη γινεσθε αφρονες. Literally, it means, "do not be ignorant." The verb is a present imperative from γινομαι, indicating a state that believers should choose to avoid. Such a choice is possible, because God has provided information sufficient for obedience. "Unwise," from αφρων, means "foolish" or "ignorant."[119] Bertram defines it as "foolish or careless conduct," contrasting it with συνιεντες ("prudent observance") in this verse.[120] This seems to indicate that the reasoning power of a believer is limited, if he does not know the will of God. In other words, clear understanding of the will of God is the antithesis of foolishness or spiritual ignorance.

---

[118] TDNT, s. v. "δοκιμος," by Walter Grundmann, vol. 2, 256.
[119] BAG, s. v. "αφρων," 127.
[120] TDNT, s. v. αφρων, αφρωνη," by Georg Bertram, vol. 9, 231.

Gaining understanding. The positive commandment in this verse is συνιεντες τι το θελημα του κυριου. Since "understanding" is the present participle form of συνιημι, it indicates a continuing action of "gaining insight into."[121] This is the metaphorical use of the root, which originally meant, "to bring together."[122] Howard has suggested that the usage here demonstrates that discerning the will of God is not always an instantaneous event, but it often involves a process of "putting together" the pieces of a puzzle.[123] This terminology better fits the idea of an individual will than it does the moral will of God.[124] The "will (θελημα) of the Lord" is the word more often

---

[121] BAG, s. v. "συνιημι," 797-798.

[122] W. E. Vine, An Expository Dictionary of New Testament Words, vol. 4, 168.

[123] Howard, 44-45.

[124] The commands in the context give principles that form part of the moral will of God. In fact, understanding the individual will of God is part of the moral will of God. However, these principles must still be "fleshed out" in specific actions ("walk circumspectly," for example, is a principle that needs to be demonstrated by actions). It is the contention here that "understanding the will of God" also must be demonstrated by specific actions. It would seem redundant for God to list several aspects of His moral will, and in the interior of that list, simply to say that the list should be understood. This reasoning appears to conclude that verse 17 is a commandment parallel to the other principles (not necessarily encompassing them). Therefore, it must refer to the individual will of God.

used for the non-determinative will of God, and is similar to
θελησις, which sometimes denotes a "wish."[125]

The introductory phrase, δια τουτο, signifying
"because of this," sheds further light upon the meaning here.
The result of displaying the spiritual diligence indicated in
verses 14-16 is the avoidance of ignorance concerning the will
of God. Paul seems to say that the spiritually diligent are those
whose minds are under God's control, resulting in their
capability to understand God's will. If the "will of the Lord"
here referred solely to God's moral will, δια τουτο would not
make much sense. The line of argument would then proceed as
follows: obey the moral will of God described in the context,
and because of this you will understand the moral will that has
been obeyed! Such a connotation surely dilutes any meaning
that verse 17 might otherwise have. When viewed as the
individual will, the commandments for spiritual diligence
simply follow the pattern of prerequisites which must be met
before the individual will is understood.

Application. Thus, the teaching of Ephesians 5:17 is
that Spirit-filled reasoning is the result of spiritual character,
and it is possible for a Godly man to avoid ignorance while

---

[125] Howard, 217.

gaining insight into the will of God. Not only is it possible, but it is required that Christians do so. This seems to indicate that God enlightens a mature Christian's thinking processes, to allow him to understand what God's will is. A similar conclusion will be drawn later in this chapter from the study of Romans 12:1-2.

<u>Colossians 1:9</u>

<u>The context</u>. A further indication of the believer's opportunity to know the will of God is given in the Apostle Paul's prayer for the believers at Colosse, as quoted in Colossians 1:9-10. Paul had heard of their testimony of faith (verse 4), love (verses 4, 8), hope (verse 5), and fruitfulness (verse 6), from Epaphras. In light of these spiritual qualities ("for this cause"), Paul prayed unceasingly that the saints in Colosse would ". . . be filled with the knowledge. . . " of God's will.

This prayer would be futile if there were not a knowable, specific plan of God for His children. The sovereign plan of God cannot be known ahead of time, and the moral will of God is revealed in the Bible. Friesen finds only the moral will of God in this passage by focusing primarily on the idea of "walking worthy," as verse 10 describes. It is his contention that the reference to a worthy walk in other Pauline passages refers to the moral will of God. Then he says:

In fact, Ephesians 4:1 introduces the section of that epistle that is devoted to moral commands concerning Christian behavior. A "worthy walk" would conform to all of the exhortations in chapters 4, 5, and 6 of Ephesians![126]

Unwittingly, Friesen has helped the cause of traditionalists by asserting that *all* of the exhortations of those three chapters are involved in the "worthy walk." Since Ephesians 5:17 includes an exhortation to understand the will of God, and since a solid case can be built for that passage referring to the individual will, the door is also open to the possibility that Colossians 1:9 is not merely limited to the moral will of God.

Full knowledge. "Filled" is the aorist subjunctive passive form of πληροω and has the connotation, "ye may be filled completely or richly."[127] It has a "strong element of exclusiveness or totality."[128] The "knowledge" spoken of is related to the verb, επιγινωσκω, which means "to know

---

[126] Friesen, 103.
[127] TDNT, s. v. "πληροω," by Gerhard Delling, vol. 6, 291.
[128] Ibid.

exactly, or completely," when the preposition makes "its influence felt."[129]

Bultmann seems to disagree, saying its general meaning is "to perceive," meaning essentially the same thing as γινωσκω, but he does acknowledge that the compound may be chosen intentionally sometimes to mean "to confirm."[130] He cites Luke 1:4, among others, as an example of this usage. In that passage, Theophilus is to gain επιγνωσις by reading the report of Luke, who had "perfect understanding." This seems to support the view of Vine, who says it refers to "exact or full knowledge . . . expressing a fuller or a full knowledge, a greater participation by the knower in the object known, thus more powerfully influencing him."[131] Further support of Vine's conclusions comes from the realization that Paul used a form of γινωσκω to describe the way that the heathen "know" God in Romans 1:21, but what they rejected in verse 28 was επιγνωσις. Since the heathen had one type of knowledge about God, but not the other, it is clear that Paul sometimes made distinctions between these two words. Eadie has said,

---

[129] BAG, s. v. "επιγινωσκω," 290.
[130] TDNT, s. v. "γινωσκω," by Rudolf Bultmann, vol. 1, 704.
[131] Vine, vol.2, 301.

"We cannot agree . . . that γνωσις and επιγνωσις have no distinction in the diction of the apostle Paul."[132]

With that Pauline precedent established, it seems in order to allow the stronger meaning for επιγινωσκω in Colossians 1:9. Even Bultmann acknowledges that, coupled with πληροω, it means "fulness (sic) of insight into the will of God."[133] Commenting on this passage, Hendriksen points out that this is not merely the abstract, sometimes mystical knowledge of γνωσις, but indicates clear knowledge.[134] The repetition of this word near the end of verse 10 reveals Paul's desire that the Colossians increase in the more nearly complete knowledge of God. Thus, two significant Greek words in verse 9 (one of which is repeated in verse 10) encourage the dominance of the will of God in the thought life of every Christian.

<u>Non-determinative</u>. Again, θεληματος is used for "will," emphasizing the likelihood that this refers to the non-determinative will of God. Friesen concludes that this speaks of the general will of God because of the phrase "walk worthy" in

---

[132] John Eadie, <u>Commentary on the Epistle of Paul to the Colossians</u>, 21.
[133] <u>TDNT</u>, Ibid.
[134] William Hendriksen, <u>Exposition of Colossians and Philemon</u>, 56-57.

verse 10.[135] However, verse 10 says that believers should know God's will, in order to please Him in ". . . every good work." This indicates the presence of detailed obedience, not just general acceptability.[136]

Mental excellence. Further evidence that God desires believers to have full understanding of His will is seen in the phrase, "in *all* wisdom and spiritual understanding." Σωφια ("wisdom") is "insight into the true nature of things."[137] It is "mental excellence in its highest and fullest sense."[138] "Understanding" is συνεσει, or "the faculty of deciding in particular cases."[139] This ability to decide is another way of describing the discernment of the will of God, enabling man to "walk worthy" of God (verse 10). As a consequence, the

---

[135] Friesen, 102-103.

[136] In the so-called "wisdom" view, the moral will, which is found totally in the Bible, places all other actions that do not conflict with it in the realm of acceptability. But this should be challenged, from the standpoint that the mere fact a given action is not *immoral* is not proof that it is *amoral*. Nor does the absence of evil works constitute the performance of "every good work."

[137] Vine, vol. 4, 221.

[138] G. Abbott-Smith, A Manual Greek Lexicon of the New Testament, 428.

[139] A. T. Robertson, The Epistles of Paul, vol. 4 of Word Pictures in the New Testament, 475.

Christian has a tremendously enhanced spiritual understanding that helps in the process of making decisions.

Application. A summary of this passage will bring the following applications: (1) the knowledge God desires His saints to have concerning His will is a fuller, more precise knowledge,[140] (2) full knowledge of God's will powerfully influences man's decisions, and (3) knowing God's will fully helps man to walk worthy of God.

Romans 12:1-2

Context. One of the key passages in all the Bible regarding the will of God is Romans 12:1-2. It has even been said that ". . . the central New Testament teaching about the subject (the will of God) is found in Romans 12:1, 2."[141] It begins a new section of thought in the book, as the subject of personal holiness is introduced. But this new thought is the

---

[140] It was to be more precise than the knowledge the Colossians had at the time of Paul's writing. It seems reasonable to conclude that the goal of Paul's prayer was not that more Bible would be written, which would be the case if this only referred to the moral will of God. He wanted the Colossians to more fully understand the details of God's plan for their individual lives and to continually increase in that knowledge (verse 10) as they grew.
[141] Coder, 69.

applicational conclusion (indicated by "therefore," in verse 1) to the theological assertions about the "unsearchable," sovereign God, whose ways are "past finding out (Romans 11:33-34)." Since man, in and of himself, cannot comprehend God, he needs the formula described in Romans 12:1-2, to find out the detailed will of God. Since man does not have to meet spiritual requirements in order to have more Bible written, the information about the will of God in these verses must have reference to the specific will of God, rather than the moral will.

Further study of the context will reveal that verses 1-2 present a unit of thought, speaking of personal consecration. Verse 3 deals with humility, verses 4-5 teach unity, and verses 6-8 mention spiritual gifts.

Friesen says that this passage speaks of the moral will of God, because the following context gives moral commands. He lists the use of spiritual gifts, love, devotion to others, diligence in service, rejoicing, hospitality, and blessing persecutors. He then concludes that there is no mention of choosing a mate or a location or ". . . anything else that is so specific as to be a part of God's individual will."[142] In his thinking, the absence of these things proves that the passage refers to the moral will of God.

---

[142] Friesen, 106.

However, all of these areas of moral will that he cites are general principles that must be acted out through specific steps. In other words, Paul is trying to mold the attitudes of the Roman believers, knowing that specific actions will result.

The moral will of God expressed in Romans 12:1-2 is to assume three attitudes: (1) present the body, (2) be not conformed to the world, and (3) be transformed. It is logical to conclude that the resultant action will be discernment of, and obedience to, the specific will of God. Such an interpretation does no violence whatever to the context.[143]

The logic of service. The first verse commands Christians to present their bodies to God, calling such dedication "reasonable service" (λογικην λατρειαν). Thus, there is "logic" in serving God. Barnes takes this phrase to mean ". . . worship that is governed by reason."[144] Strathmann agrees, defining it as ". . . a service of God which corresponds to

---

[143] Again, Friesen fails to take into account the fact that the command to know the individual will of God is part of the moral will of God. Even with that understanding, the reference to knowing the will of God is not an imperative in Romans 12:1-2, but describes what will *result* from obeying the moral will of God. This result is not more Bible being written, but rather, specific guidance.
[144] Albert Barnes, 640.

human reason, in which, however, divine reason is also at work."[145]

Avoiding compromise. In verse 2, the first commandment is that believers stop fashioning themselves to this present age. The KJV uses "conformed" as the translation of συσχηματιζεσθε, which is the present middle imperative form of a root that means, "to form, or mold after."[146] It refers to external shaping, rather than to internal change.[147] The "world" is αιωνι, ". . . an age, a period of time, marked in the N. T. (*sic*) usage by spiritual or moral characteristics."[148] Clarke defines it as ". . . the customs and fashions of the people who then lived."[149] It follows, then, that God is warning Christians to avoid pursuing external fashions and customs of a pagan culture that would tend to limit their consecration to Christ.

Internal change. A contrasting thought is introduced by the particle, αλλα. Rather than being externally affected by surrounding culture, Christians are to μεταμορφουσθε ("be

---

[145] TDNT, s. v. "λατρεια," by H. Strathmann, vol. 4, 65.
[146] BAG, s. v. "συσχηματιζω," 803.
[147] Vine, Vol. 1, 227.
[148] Ibid., vol. 4, 233.
[149] Adam Clarke, Romans to the Revelations, vol. 2 of The New Testament of our Lord and Savior Jesus Christ, 137.

transforming yourselves"). Grammatically parallel to the previous imperative, this connotes an inward change.[150] Agreeing that the "metamorphosis" is an internal alteration, Vine adds that it ". . . will find expression in character and conduct."[151]

This is an internal change, because it is produced by a mind renewal (ανακαινωσει του νοος). "Renewal" is described as ". . . the adjustment of the moral and spiritual vision and thinking to the mind of God, which is designed to have a transforming effect upon the life."[152] Νοος refers to ". . . the power to arrive at moral judgments."[153] A broadened definition allows this word to encompass perception, understanding, feeling, judging, and deciding.[154] It is the internal, reflective part of man, then, that is to undergo the "metamorphosis" demanded here.[155]

---

[150] BAG, s. v. "μεταμορφεω," 513.

[151] Vine, vol. 4, 148.

[152] Ibid., vol. 3, 279.

[153] BAG, s. v. "νοος," 546.

[154] Vine, vol. 3, 69.

[155] The change in a believer's internal reflective consciousness is produced by the instrumentality of God's Word. Psalm 119:9-11 teaches the effectiveness of the Word for combating sin.

Friesen correctly notes that ". . . it is specifically the Word of God (His moral will) that effects that spiritual metamorphosis."[156] It is unfortunate that, seeing the moral will of God implied in the "mind renewal," Friesen gives it a redundant application in the following phrase. If boiled down to its elements, Friesen's concept of this passage limits God to saying that the believer's mind is renewed by the moral will of God, in order that the believer might approve of the moral will of God that has already transformed him. There appears to be no purpose in such a statement. Simple logic indicates that in order for a believer to allow the moral will of God to renew his mind, he must have *already approved* of it. He certainly needs no further tests to discern what it says!

Test and approve. All of these changes are to take place "in order that" (εις το plus the infinitive) the saints may "prove" what is the will of God. The idea of "prove" is from δοκιμαζειν, meaning ". . . to examine and approve of the results."[157] A special usage of this term is seen by Grundmann: "Christians . . . are to test or prove what is the will of God. If they are to be approved, they must do the will of God. But to

---

Friesen, 107.
[157] BAG, s. v. "δοκιμαζω," 201.

do it, they must know it by testing."[158] It is a word that was used often in reference to the tempering of metals through severe fires.[159] In application, ". . . the believer whose mind is being renewed is programmed to process data from his life—to test it, in order to discover what the will of God is."[160] Of course, the will (θελημα) of God is asserted to be ". . . good, acceptable, and perfect . . . . " Thus, the believer who discerns the will of God is also expected to approve of it and benefit from it.

Detailed plan. The last word in the verse is τελειον, which signifies completeness.[161] In passages such as Colossians 4:12, it means "fully developed."[162] This does not appear to be simply a mass of general information which leaves individual Christians to depend upon their own resources of wisdom to fill in the gaps. Each Christian is offered the opportunity to discover that complete, fully-developed plan of the omniscient God.

---

[158] TDNT, s. v. "δοκιμος," by Walter Grundmann, vol. 2, 260.
[159] Barnes, 640.
[160] Howard, 36.
[161] Vine, vol. 3, 174.
[162] BAG, s. v. "τελειος," 817.

In an attempt to bypass this significant passage, Friesen concludes that, since there are commands from God in the twelfth chapter, this must refer to the moral will of God, rather than any individual plan.[163] It must be objected, however, that δοκιμαζειν has an experimental nature, which should eliminate its application to the Word of God. The moral will of God does not come in response to man's right actions, because the revelation of Scripture is not contingent upon man. Friesen himself acknowledges that the word means "trying to learn" in Ephesians 5:10.[164] If this will were already revealed in Scripture, one would not have to "test." There would be no experiments to run!

Application. The chief ideas that can be gleaned from Romans 12:1-2, with regard to the will of God, can be summarized in this way: (1) separation from the world and consecration to Christ result in the believer's capability to discover God's specific will, (2) God works to internalize His will, by renewing man's mind, (3) Christians with renewed minds can test and approve of the will of God, and (4) God's plan for the believer is fully developed.

---

[163] Friesen, 106.
[164] Ibid., 107.

Romans 8:14

Special leading of the Lord is not limited to just a few unique Bible characters of ancient history, nor even to a few exceptionally dedicated Christians today. It is the statement of Romans 8:14 that the leadership of the Holy Spirit is one of the evidences of true salvation.

The context. The first twenty-five verses of chapter eight of Romans conclude a section of the book that deals with sanctification. It is directed to Christians (verse 1), and they are challenged to avoid carnality (verses 5-9). The dangers of fleshliness are pointed out in verse 13, where the believer is instructed to "mortify," or "put to death," (θανατουτε) the flesh.[165] Thus, the statement in verse 14 regarding the leading of the Holy Spirit appears, as is so often the case, after a challenge to strengthen one's personal relationship with the Lord.

In fairness, this verse is debatable, as far as its application to the individual will of God is concerned. There are indicators that seem to allow such an application, but the passage does not appear to give sufficient information to force that conclusion.

---

[165] BAG, s. v. "θανατοω," 352.

However, it does not give solid backing for the "wisdom" school, either. Friesen denies its applicability to the individual will by saying that the context does not deal with ". . . daily decision making in nonmoral areas."[166] If that were the criterion for validity, Friesen would have great difficulty with James 1:5—one of the foundational passages on wisdom— for its context also fails to mention such decisions. Friesen says, "Neither the verse itself nor the near context give any indication that the *means* (emphasis his) of the leading is by 'inward impressions.'"[167] It should be pointed out that Romans 8:14 does not mention *wisdom*, or even the *Bible*, as the means of that leading either! If a position can be refuted solely by an argument from silence, then those who see only the moral will of God in Romans 8 might do well to consider the curious absence of imperative verbs in that chapter. Since Friesen discounts the possibility of the individual will of God in other passages whose contexts *include* imperatives, what justification does he have for drawing the same conclusion when imperatives are not found?

Romans 8:14, standing alone, would not prove the entire "peace" system of discerning the will of God, but there is

---

[166] Friesen, 137.
[167] Ibid.

certainly nothing in the verse or in its context that refutes that
view either. Its consideration here simply shows its
compatibility with the traditional position.

Every believer's experience. The experience described
in verse 14 is said to be applicable to all Christians. The word
οσοι, used of quantity and number, means "every one who" in
this passage.[168] "Leading" is a translation of αγονται, which is a
present indicative passive verb. It is a figurative usage, from
αγω, which means "to lead, guide."[169] Thus, every believer is
being led, or guided. The leading of the Holy Spirit in this
verse is an internal leading, just as the witness of the Spirit in
verse 16 is an internal witness. The verse does not elaborate on
the specifics of that leading, but it certainly asserts that
guidance will be the experience of every believer. The
following statement by Barnes seems to summarize it:

> The apostle here does not agitate the question *how* it is
> that the people of God are led by the Spirit, or why
> they yield to it when others resist it. His design is
> simply to state the fact, that they who *are* thus led are

---

[168] BAG, s. v. "οσος," 590.
[169] Ibid., s. v. "αγω," 14.

the sons of God, or have evidence of piety (emphasis his).[170]

An opposite view. Friesen says that the traditional view does not work with immature Christians, who may foolishly rush into some action that they feel God has led them to take. He rightly observes, "Immature believers tend to make immature decisions—at least with a higher degree of frequency than more mature saints."[171] But it must be said that the problem of immaturity also plagues Friesen's view, since the immature believer lacks the depth of wisdom and Bible knowledge required to make decisions.

There is no shortcut to finding the will of God. The same immature believer who thinks God led him to a choice that others see as foolish, might just as easily lift a verse of Scripture out of context and make an equally foolish choice, if he follows Friesen's view. Both the "peace" and "wisdom" views require believers to be mature in the decision making process, but the abuse by immature believers does not disprove the method legitimately used by the mature.

---

[170] Barnes, 605.
[171] Friesen, 123.

Application. A few conclusions can be made from this verse. First, the leading of the Holy Spirit is an evidence of salvation. Second, the Holy Spirit works on believers internally. Third, the internal ministry of the Holy Spirit results in guidance for every believer. Logic would add that the more sensitive one is to the Holy Spirit, the more he will understand and benefit from that guidance, since the Holy Spirit can be "quenched" (I Thessalonians 5:19) and "grieved" (Ephesians 4:30) by carnal Christians.

II Corinthians 10:5

The topic of knowing God's will cannot be thoroughly studied without considering how God works within the Christian to reveal specific details. It is not that the believer never uses his rational faculties. The truth is that those faculties are yielded to God, then God directs by controlling the thoughts of that yielded mind. Thus, the charge is to bring ". . . into captivity every thought to the obedience of Christ," according to the instruction of II Corinthians 10:5. Nelson explains God's inner working as both direct and indirect control of man's thought life. He says:

> God can exercise an indirect control over our minds by maintaining principles, psychological in nature, which regulate the functioning of the mind. Since He controls circumstances which produce psychological effects upon us, and since He controls the principles governing

the mind's functioning, He can thus control the mind. . . . God exercises a certain amount of direct control over men's thoughts and actions. He is able to cause a man's mind to have a certain thought just as He is able to do anything else He pleases, since He is omnipotent (see Rev. 17:17).[172]

The context. Chapters 8-10 of II Corinthians form a section that speaks of spiritual dedication, specifically illustrated in the use of money. There is an example of sacrificial giving on the part of the Macedonian churches (8:1-5), followed by the statement that giving proves the sincerity of one's love (8:8). Chapter 8 continues to point out the importance of equity and honesty in finances, and chapter 9 gives instruction for advance preparations in giving (verses 1-5).

In an attempt to condition the minds of the readers concerning giving, Paul makes several assertions that contradict the thinking processes of the selfish. Whereas man supposes that he will have more by hoarding, God says that bountiful sowing results in bountiful reaping (9:6). Man expects that through giving his resources will be reduced. However, Paul speaks of God's ability to multiply the seed sown (9:10).

---

[172] Nelson, 16-17.

Whereas man thinks in the physical realm, Paul says that the Christian's "war" and "weapons" are not of the flesh (10:3-4).

It is at this point that Paul explains in verse 5 how God can take the yielded mind of a believer and make his thoughts obedient. It requires the ". . . pulling down of strong holds" (verse 4), indicating the enormity of the process of rejecting human philosophies.[173] The ultimate results of that obedience in the thought life, of course, will be the expanded faith of the Christian and the increased spread of the Gospel (10:15-16).

Wrong thinking. The first portion of verse 5 has to do with the rejection of wrong thought processes. Christians are told to be "Casting down imaginations . . . . " (λογισμους καθαιρουντες). Λογισμους refers to reasoning or thought, often with an evil intent.[174] The Greek philosophers placed a great value upon logical procedures, but ". . . they were obliged to *assume principles* which were either such as did not exist, or were false in themselves (emphasis his)."[175] It is aptly said that,

---

[173] Clark, 355.
[174] Vine, vol. 2, 248.
[175] Clarke, Ibid.

"The foes of Christianity pretend to a great deal of *reason*, and rely on that in resisting the gospel (emphasis his)."[176]

The participle is present passive, from καθαιρεω. The basic meaning of this word is to "tear down," and the figurative usage here means to "destroy."[177] While Christianity is not an unreasoning system, it depends upon an enlightened reasoning power, available to the believer through the indwelling Holy Spirit. Christianity therefore rejects the humanistic rationalism that spawns infidelity.

Humanistic pride. Humanism seems to be the contemporary target of the phrase "every high thing," of which Barnes says: "Every exalted opinion respecting the dignity and purity of human nature; all the pride of the human heart and of the understanding."[178] The Greek term, υψωμα, evidently uses "high" in the sense of the exaltation of pride.[179] It is this pride which "exalteth itself" (εκαιρομενον). This is a present middle participle, so it connotes action that is continual and reflects back upon the subject ("itself"). This self-exaltation is directed against the νγωσις ("knowledge") of God. The obvious

---

[176] Barnes, 886.
[177] BAG, s. v. "καθαιρεω," 387.
[178] Barnes, Ibid.
[179] BAG, s. v. "υψωμα," 858.

conclusion is that the self-exaltation of humanistic pride detracts from one's ability to reason accurately concerning God.

Captive thoughts. Having rejected the negatives, the believer who wants to know God's will must add some very positive principles to his thinking process. The phrase, αιχμαλωτιζοντες παν νοημα, is translated, ". . . bringing into captivity every thought. . . . " The verb form is another present participle, appearing this time in the active voice. The root means to ". . . capture, as in war."[180] It is derived from αιχμη, for "spear," and αλωτος, translated "capture."[181] Thus, the original idea of the compound was, "to capture with a spear." In his search for the specific will of God, the Christian must realize that there is a spiritual "warring" for his mind. Christ wants to capture it (with the "spear" of obedience).

Νοημα ("mind") has the connotation of "thought, purpose, or plot."[182] "Obedience" is υπακοην, signifying ". . . the obedience which every slave owes his master."[183] Barnes applies it this way: "All the *plans of life* should be controlled by

---

[180] BAG, s. v. "αιχμαλωτιζω," 26.
[181] Vine, vol. 1, 167.
[182] BAG, s. v. "νοημα," 542.
[183] Ibid., 844.

the will of Christ, and formed and executed under his control—
as captives are led by a conqueror (emphasis his)."[184]

    <u>Application</u>. In order to know the specific will of God,
it is important for the believer to heed the instructions of II
Corinthians 10:5. Several principles can be gleaned from this
portion. First, it is necessary to reject wrong thought processes,
since human philosophy hinders one's ability to understand
God. Second, Christianity uses a system of logic that depends
upon enlightened reasoning power, available through the
indwelling presence of the Holy Spirit. Third, humanistic
reasoning is motivated by pride and exalts itself. Fourth,
humanistic rationalism exalts itself at the expense of the full
knowledge of God. Fifth, the obedient Christian must establish
some positive Biblical principles in his thought process. Sixth,
there is a spiritual warfare for man's mind, and the believer who
wants to be victorious must surrender his mind as Christ's
"captive." These principles, when applied to an individual's life,
will direct his thoughts so he can better discern the specific will
of God. Thus, when he makes decisions, the believer will have
confidence that God is in control.

---

[184] Barnes, 886.

<u>Colossians 4:12.</u>

A ministry of intercession assists others in the understanding of God's will. In Colossians 4:12, the prayers of Epaphras, the probable founder of the church at Colosse,[185] were helpful in the achievement of God's will by his flock. Paul says:

> Epaphras, who is one of you, a servant of Christ, saluteth you, always labouring fervently for you in prayers, that ye may stand perfect and complete in all the will of God.

<u>The context</u>. The book of Colossians shows that Christ is sufficient for victorious Christian living. Chapter 1 speaks of the accomplishments of Christ in behalf of the Christian. Chapter 2 points out His sufficiency to combat pagan philosophies and lifestyles. In chapter 3 the believer is urged to imitate Christ's principles of life. Chapter 4 describes His ministry, challenging the saints to be able to ". . . answer every man . . . . (verse 6)."

Verse 12 appears in an immediate context of salutations by Paul in behalf of various servants of God to the church.

---

[185] Hendriksen, 15.

Epaphras, who had traveled at least one thousand miles—
perhaps as many as thirteen hundred, depending upon which
route he took—to visit Paul in a Roman prison,[186] is included in
the greeting.

Intercessory prayer. Epaphras is said to have fervently
prayed for the Colossians regarding the will of God. Friesen
seems correct in his assumption that Epaphras prayed for the
same thing that Paul petitioned for in Colossians 1:9.[187]
However, that is not necessarily the moral will, as Friesen
concludes.[188] Since Epaphras prayed that the Colossians would

---

[186] Ibid., 16.

[187] Friesen, 105.

[188] Friesen bases his conclusions on Colossians 4:12 upon his conclusions
from 1:9, which, in turn, are based upon his opinions of Ephesians 5:17.
Since there does not seem to be convincing evidence for his viewpoint
of Ephesians 5:17, it seems that a "domino effect" could take place with
regard to the passages in Colossians. Again, he seems to find only the
moral will of God in these Scriptures by virtue of a circular pattern of
thought. On page 105, his explanation of Paul's desire to produce
spiritual maturity in the believers at Colosse lacks proof. He states that
"Paul was bringing the moral will of God to bear upon the lives of those
to whom he had ministered to bring them to maturity." He then asserts
that the will which Paul and Epaphras desired for the Colossians to be
dominated by must also be the moral will. This is another passage that
can be seen in a different light if it is understood that part of God's
moral will is to know and obey His individual will. The idea of a "will

stand τελειοι ("complete") in the will of God, it is reasonable to assume he desired for them that will which Romans 12:2 describes as τελειον. It has already been seen in this chapter that there is good reason to see the individual will in Romans 12:2.[189] Epaphras' "labor" in prayer is αγωνιζομενος, meaning "while wrestling." The initial idea was ". . . to contend in the gymnastic games, to contend with adversaries. . . ."[190] Thus, the seriousness of doing God's will is such that agonizing prayer is an important part of the process. In this case, the agonizing was performed as a ministry of intercession for others.

---

within a will" is not totally foreign to Friesen, since his figure on page 232 reveals that all actions done in fulfillment of the moral will of God are also within the sovereign will of God. It would seem appropriate to modify the model to include the individual will of God inside the "area of freedom" Friesen describes.

[189] Of Romans 12:2, Friesen admits (page 106) that both the context and the use of δοκομαζειν ". . . will fit either the moral or individual senses of God's will." He then goes on to contradict himself by implying that the individual will does *not* fit the context. Since Friesen denies that the individual will even exists, it seems that the burden of proof is upon him. Therefore, if even *one* passage of Scripture can possibly refer to the individual will, then his view cannot be espoused with dogmatism.

[190] Kenneth S. Wuest, Mark—Romans—Galatians—Ephesians and Colossians, vol. 1 of Wuest's Word Studies from the Greek New Testament, 237.

Standing perfect. The laborious prayers of Epaphras implored God that the Colossians would "stand perfect" (στητε τελειοι) in God's will. The verb is an aorist subjunctive, which indicates the possibility of accomplishment. That is, it was possible for the Colossians to "stand" in the desired condition, and Epaphras wanted to see that condition actualized. The root is ιστημι, which here has the metaphorical usage, "stand firm."[191] Τελειοι means "totality," and here ". . . is referring to the solid position occupied by Christians as those who are 'whole'. . . in the total will of God."[192]

Standing complete. Epaphras also prayed that the saints in Colosse would stand "complete" (πεπληρωμενοι) in God's will. This word is a perfect passive participle, from πληροω, meaning "having been made full."[193] Both Paul and Epaphras see the will (θεληματι) of God as that which brings fullness of understanding to the believer. This seems to indicate detailed, rather than partial, information given by God to Christians.

Application. Several principles about the non-determinative will of God can be discerned from a study of this passage. First, understanding the will of God sometimes requires

---

[191] Vine, vol. 4, 70.
[192] TDNT, s. v. "τελειος," by Gerhard Delling, vol. 8, 73-75.
[193] BAG, s. v. "πληροω," 677.

agonizing prayer. Then, assurance of the will of God encourages man to "stand firm." Third, the will of God brings wholeness to believers. Fourth, the will of God provides full understanding.

Doing God's Will

It is not enough just to know what God wants His children to do. There must also be an understanding of how to accomplish that which He desires. Thankfully, God has not left man to his own understanding, nor to his own resources, for achievement. There are several Scripture passages that concern themselves with the "how to" aspect of doing God's will. The first to be considered is Hebrews 13:21.

Hebrews 13:21

The indication of Hebrews 13:21 is that it is God Who accomplishes His will through Christians. It is prayed here that God might make believers ". . . perfect in every good work . . .," and that He would work in them to perform that which pleases Him. Thus, the performance of the will of God is actually initiated and accomplished by God Himself.

The context. The thirteenth chapter of Hebrews gives instruction for the believer's sanctification. In fact, verse 12 identifies that as the purpose for the suffering of Jesus. The writer speaks of sexual purity in verse 4 and enjoins submission to Godly leadership in verses 7 and 17. In addition to the warning against covetousness in verse 5, he has dealt with all the basic areas of worldly temptation identified in I John 2:16.[194] There is a challenge to maintain doctrinal purity (verse 9) and an encouragement to continually thank and praise God (verse 15). The following context urges the readers to listen to the word of exhortation, which had been written to them. Having dealt with the spiritual prerequisites for knowing the will of God, he offers a prayer in verses 20-21 for the believers to be perfected in that will.

Although Friesen does not show exegesis of this verse, he lists it with several others, evidently implying that they all clearly refer to the moral will of God.[195] In fact, while it is immediately evident that I Thessalonians 4:1-2 refers to the moral will, the other passages could all be questioned in that regard, including Hebrews 13:21.

Perfection. As is so often the case in the New Testament when the will of God is dealt with, spiritual prerequisites are mentioned. The term ". . . make you perfect . . ." again appears in this verse. That word in the Greek is καταρτισαι, from a compound root with an interesting derivation. Clarke has this to say of its related noun form.

---

[194] The "lust of the flesh" speaks of body appetites, the "lust of the eye" evidently refers to materialism (cf Proverbs 28:22; 22:9; Ecclesiastes 4:8), and the "pride of life" is self-explanatory.
[195] Friesen, 110.

Καταρτισις, from κατα, *intensive*, and αρτιζω, to *fit* or *adapt*, signifies the reducing of a *dislocated limb* to its proper place . . . . It is a metaphor, also, taken from a *building*; the several *stones* and *timbers* being all put in their proper places and situations, so that the whole building might be *complete* . . . (emphasis his)."[196]

Barnes says the word means ". . . to make fully ready, to put in full order; to make complete,"[197] while Wuest assigns the meaning, ". . . to equip one for service."[198] Vine's definition of this word is ". . . to render fit . . . ," signifying ". . . right ordering and arrangement."[199] Arndt and Gingich translate it ". . . put into proper condition."[200] The idea, then, is that this is a strong word describing very positive benefits to the Christian. The prayer put forth by the writer of Hebrews is that the saints would not lack any part of the spiritual equipment needed to do God's will.

Good works. The full equipment is intended to result in every "good work" (εργω αγαθω) being accomplished in the Christian. This can include ". . . every activity undertaken for

---

[196] Clarke, 374.

[197] Barnes, 1344.

[198] Kenneth S. Wuest, Philippians—Hebrews—The Pastoral Epistles— First Peter—In These Last Days, vol. 2 of Wuest's Word Studies From the Greek New Testament, 242.

[199] Vine, vol. 3, 174.

[200] BAG, s. v. "καταρτιζω," 418.

Christ's sake."[201] Αγαθω designates that which is ". . .
intrinsically valuable, morally good."[202]

Doing God's Will. The actual doing of God's will is
accomplished by God Himself. First, He equips the believer to do
His will, then He works in the believer that which is "well
pleasing" in His sight. The first aspect is indicated by the phrase,
εις το ποιησαι ("in order to do") His θελημα. It is evident that
there is nothing lacking in the provision that God has made for
believers. Hence, they have the full capability to accomplish His
will.

The second aspect is seen from the words, ποιων εν υμιν
("working in you"). Whereas both words for "you" in this verse
are plural, signifying a general audience of believers, ποιων is a
present participle with a masculine *singular* ending. Clearly, God
is the subject, with the present participial form indicating action
that is simultaneous with that of the main verb ("make you
perfect"). Therefore, while God is in the process of equipping the
saints, he is actively "doing" in them that which pleases Himself.
This makes it possible for man to "do" God's will.

The idea here is, that the only hope that they would do the
will of God was, that *he* would, by his own agency, cause

---

[201] Vine, 231.
[202] BAG, s. v. "αγαθος," 3.

them to do what was well-pleasing in his sight . . . . It is not from any expectation that man would do it himself.[203]

The work of God in believers is ευαρεστων, which allows man's work to be "acceptable" to God.[204] Thus, man is not limited to his own understanding of spiritual matters, nor to his own natural resources in the accomplishment of them.

Application. The conclusions drawn from Hebrews 13:21 reveal why God's expectations of believers are realistic. He not only gives them knowledge of His will, but he enables them to fulfill it. The first principle to note is that God fully equips His children to please Him. Second, Christians have the God-given potential to engage in activities that are intrinsically valuable. Third, God does the work within believers, while He is in the process of perfecting them. Fourth, God's work allows believers to please Him.

Philippians 2:13

Another significant passage which teaches how to do the will of God is Philippians 2:13. It speaks of the fact that God works within the believer, affecting both the "willing" and the "doing" of His will. The KJV translates it this way: "For it is God which worketh in you both to will and to do of his good pleasure."

---

[203] Barnes, 1344.
[204] BAG, s. v. "ευαρεστος," 319.

Even Friesen agrees that ". . . as we work through the process of arriving at a decision, God is continually present and working within us."[205]

In light of this verse, one writer has said:

The Christian should not become so preoccupied with what he should or shouldn't do that he forgets to notice what God is energizing him to want to do. God will cause us to want to do the right thing.[206]

The context. Philippians is a book that encourages rejoicing in all circumstances in life. The key verse is 4:4. Chapter two focuses attention upon the Christian's mind as one specific place to experience that joy. Paul here encourages likemindedness (verse 2), lowly mindedness (verse 3), and Christ-like mindedness (verse 5). He exalts the lowly-minded Christ (verses 9-11) and commands Christians to "work out" their faith in the Savior (verse 12). This requirement is justified by the concept in verse 13 that God works within the believer to desire and accomplish His will.

The following context speaks of attitudes and actions which allow the saint of God to keep a pure testimony before God and man (verses 14-16). The focus in this chapter on the believer's mind emphasizes the internal aspect of the will of God. The moral

---

[205] Friesen, 253.
[206] Nelson, 56.

106

will is given to man in an external form (the Bible), but this portion of God's will is communicated from God to man internally, so it must refer to the individual will.[207]

Work out. The command in verse 12 to "work out" the believer's own salvation does not detract from the doctrine of salvation by grace. Paul is not saying that salvation can be *earned* this way, but rather that it can be *demonstrated* in this way. The verb is κατεργαζεσθε, a present imperative deponent from κατεργαζομαι. The root ". . . signifies to work out, achieve, effect by toil."[208] Though Hendriksen is somewhat confused about this verse,[209] he properly says that ". . . we do not go amiss when we say that the *tense* of the verb indicates that Paul has in mind *continuous, sustained, strenuous effort* (emphasis his) . . . ."[210] Robertson says this compound word signifies to ". . . work on to

---

[207] It seems unfair of Friesen to acknowledge that God works internally upon the believer to provide *wisdom* for decision making, but at the same time to accuse traditionalists of being "subjective" because they believe God can work internally to provide *peace* for decision making.
[208] Vine, vol. 4, 232.
[209] Hendriksen says, "Believers are not saved at one stroke. Their salvation is a *process* (emphasis his)." He should notice that Paul was not telling the Philippians *how to become* Christians in 2:12, for he had already addressed them as "saints" in 1:1. It is evidential growth in the will of God that is a process.
[210] William Hendriksen, Exposition of Philippians, 120.

the finish."[211] The "working out" is the constant effort of a Christian to maintain a testimony of faithfulness to God, proving the reality of his faith by the quality of perseverance.

Working in. The command for believers to sustain an effort for God is validated by the fact that ". . . it is God which worketh in you . . . ," according to verse 13. This word for "work" is ενεργων, meaning "effectual working."[212] It is a present active participle. Hence, the time of this action is simultaneous with the action of the main verb (the command for believers to "work out"). Thus, God works internally within the believer, giving the saint the capability to work outwardly. It is an internal ministry of God, not an objective source of general revelation.

To will and to do. God's work within the Christian affects not only what the believer *does* (ενεργειν), but also what he *desires* (θελειν). Literally, God "energizes" man's will and "energy."[213] That is, He influences what man desires, then He provides the energy for the accomplishment of that desire. Clarke puts it this way:

---

[211] Robertson, 446.

[212] Marvin R. Vincent, Romans—Corinthians—Ephesians--Philippians—Colossians—Philemon, vol. 3 of Word Studies in the New Testament, 438.

[213] Robertson, 446.

The *power* to *will* and the *power* to *act* must necessarily come from God, who is the author both of the *soul* and *body*, and of all their powers and energies, but the *act* of *volition* and the *act* of *working* comes from the *man*. God gives *power* to will, man wills through that power. Without the *power* to *will*, man can *will nothing*; without the *power* to *work*, man can *do nothing*. God neither wills *for* man nor *works* in *man's stead*, but he furnishes him with power to do both; he is therefore accountable to God for these powers (emphasis his).[214]

His good pleasure. The "good pleasure" of God is His ευδοκιας ("good will").[215] Hendriksen comments:

It is *for the sake of* and *with a view to the execution of* God's good pleasure that God, as the infinite Source of spiritual and moral energy for believers, causes them to work out their own salvation (emphasis his)."[216]

Application. This passage on the will of God supplies several general principles. First, the process of doing God's will begins with God's work within the believer. Second, the reality of man's salvation is demonstrated by his continuous effort to work

---

[214] Clarke, 497.
[215] BAG, s. v. "ευδοκιας," 319.
[216] Hendriksen, 123.

for God. Third, God energizes the believer, both to desire and to perform His will.[217]

Ephesians 6:6

Still further information regarding how to do the will of God is found in Ephesians 6:6: "Not with eyeservice, as menpleasers; but as the servants of Christ, doing the will of God from the heart." The essence is that the will of God must be done from man's innermost being, as unto the Lord.

The context. The book of Ephesians has much to say about the will of God. The general will is mentioned in 1:9; the sovereign will in 1:11, and the non-determinative will in 5:17 and 6:6-7. Submission to others is enjoined in 5:21, beginning with a series of commandments concerning human relationships: the husband-wife connection (5:22-33), the parent-child relationship (6:1-4), and the servant-master affiliation (6:5-9). This instruction appears in the midst of the servant-master section. While this portion could refer to the moral will of God, the internal aspect of the response gives sufficient reason to consider it here.

---

[217] This is yet another argument for the existence of the individual will of God. If God does not have any preferences concerning those decisions made within the moral will, why would He bother to internally assist man's will? If God works upon man's will, it must be because God wants that will to be exercised in a certain direction. Since Friesen relates this verse to the process of decision making (page 253), it is surprising that he overlooks this passage in his exegetical work.

Eyeservice. In this passage Paul gives servants a proper motivation to work for their masters. First, that motivation is considered negatively, ". . . not with eyeservice." This word is οφθαλμοδουλειαν, which ". . . denotes service performed only under the master's eye . . . diligently performed when he is looking, but neglected in his absence."[218] The same idea is seen in the usage of ανθρωπαρεσκοι ("one who tries to please men at the sacrifice of principle").[219] God clearly abhors the kind of work that stems from a strictly external motivation, producing self-gratification.

Soul-service. The right motivation for external work is an internal spiritual condition that honors God. Christian workers are really the "servants" (δουλοι) of God. They are to do the will (θελημα) of God from the ψυχης, which means "soul," in the sense of the ". . . seat and center of the inner life of man."[220] Thus, the inner life of man provides the motivation for doing the will of God. This is not a strictly objective activity but actually stems from man's innermost being. This, of course, is diametrically opposed to the external motive of "eyeservice."

Application. The motivation for doing the will of God does not come from the external man. It is not merely intended to

---

[218] Vine, vol. 2, 65.
[219] BAG, s. v. "ανθρωπαρεσκος," 67.
[220] Ibid., s. v. "ψυχη," 901.

be that which matters only when seen by men. It is rightly performed when it stems from the inner being of man and is done as unto the Lord. Thus, doing the will of God is an internalized obedience that results in external activity.

Colossians 3:15

The final text to be studied in the consideration of how to do the will of God is Colossians 3:15: "And let the peace of God rule in your hearts . . . ." This verse emphasizes the internalization of the will of God and instructs believers to allow the peace of God to arbitrate in their decisions.

The context. In the previous study of Colossians 1:9-10, the context of the book has been considered. At this point, the focus will be upon chapter 3, which encourages believers to imitate the principles of Christ. The first four verses challenge Christians to appropriate, in practical living, their positions in Christ. Next, there is a reminder that they have been delivered from fleshliness and sensuality (verses 5-7), followed by a challenge to "put off" that which is wrong and "put on" that which honors God (verses 8-14).

Verses 15-16 give two resources for guidance in the lives of believers—the peace of God and the Word of God. Friesen strongly asserts that ". . . any interpretation of Colossians 3:15 that explains it in terms of inner guidance in normal decision making is absolutely foreign to the context."[221] However, verse 16, which seems to "couple" with verse 15 by parallel phrases ("let peace rule" and "let the Word dwell"), speaks of "wisdom," which doubtless is to be used in making decisions.[222] Both peace and the Word are to be appropriated internally and should be motivating factors in the believers' minds.

Ruling peace. The instruction of verse 15 is to allow the ειρηνη ("sense of rest and contentment")[223] from God to direct believers. This peace finds its true foundation in a proper spiritual relationship with God. It has been said that:

> No heart is right with God where the *peace of Christ* does not rule; and the continual prevalence of the peace of

---

[221] Friesen, 142.

[222] It is not unprecedented for Paul to mention "peace" in a way that seems disjointed from its surrounding context. For some examples, see Romans 16:20; Galatians 6:16; and II Thessalonians 3:16. In fact, the kind of "peace" that Paul included as a greeting in every one of his signed epistles is not clarified by contextual statements. It should also be noted that the challenge to "be thankful" appears disjointed in the context of Colossians 3:15. It is a reasonable conclusion to see the "peace" of this verse as relating to interpersonal problems, but Paul still says that "peace" (rather than statements in the Bible) should act as an "arbitrator." Obviously, arbitration involves the making of decisions within certain guidelines. Such a position does not conflict with individual guidance.

[223] Clarke, 528.

Christ is the decisive proof that the heart *is* right with God
.... While peace rules, all is safe (emphasis his)."[224]

The word "rule" is used metaphorically. It is βραβευετω,
an imperative form of βραβευω, ". . . to act as an umpire."[225]
Stauffer gives the following insight:

> Common from the time of Euripides, this word refers
> originally to the activity of the umpire . . . whose office at
> the games is to direct, arbitrate, and decide the contest. In
> the wider sense it then comes to mean "to order," "rule,"
> or "control."[226]

Of the ruling "umpire" of peace from God, one author has
stated:

> The word "peace" means a state of harmony and inner
> tranquility. It is that feeling we have when things are all
> right. . . . This word "rule" refers to the activity of the
> umpire at an athletic contest. He makes the decisions. He
> settles the disputes.[227]

Another commentator says:

---

[224] Ibid.
[225] Robertson, 505.
[226] TDNT, s. v. "βραβευω," by Ethelbert Stauffer, vol. 1, 637-638.
[227] Howard, 89-90.

"Peace" is commonly with the apostle a far higher blessing than mere harmony with others, or the study of Christian union. It is with him synonymous with happiness, that calm of mind which is not ruffled by adversity, overclouded by sin or a remorseful conscience, or disturbed by the fear and the approach of death. . . . This peace was to possess undisputed supremacy—was to be uncontrolled president in their hearts.[228]

Ruling heart. To prove that there is no Scriptural validity in ridiculing the "subjectivity" of the traditional view of God's will, the teaching here is that "umpiring peace" should control men's καρδιαις ("hearts"). This is yet another word expressing internalization, denoting the ". . . center and source of the whole inner life, with its thinking, feeling, and volition."[229] Since this peace is to rule their "hearts," it is an *inner* "peace." When inward peace controls, there will most likely also be a resultant outward peace in the home, church, and other human relationships. But even if outward peace does not exist, it is still possible for individuals to have inner peace.

In Romans 14 Paul speaks of issues that are not included in the moral will of God, in which individuals have to make decisions. In verses 5 and 23, he indicates that the individual who

---

[228] Eadie, 247, 249.
[229] BAG, s. v. "καρδια," 404.

participates in a given activity is sinning if he lacks assurance of its correctness. This is one way that peace (in this case, the lack of it) "rules" in one's heart when decisions are made.

Application. There are principles here concerning the will of God which are germane to this study. It must be first reiterated that doing the will of God is an internalized experience for the believer. Second, God gives peace to those who are in His will. Third, that peace is an inner sense of rest and contentment which gives assurance about God's direction. Fourth, God's peace acts as an internal "umpire" for man. Fifth, man's outward conflicts are to be dealt with by the arbitration of Christ's peace within. Sixth, the Christian is supposed to allow that peace to direct him. With this internal "umpire," every Christian could have the direction to do the will of God. Of course, he must meet the spiritual prerequisites that allow him to qualify for such guidance, or he will not have the "umpiring" peace.

Summary

The New Testament gives abundant instruction regarding how to know and do the will of God. It is clear that God has a specific plan for individuals, which is demonstrated by several supporting arguments. The Ephesian Christians were commanded to understand the will of God (Ephesians 5:17), so it is sin not to do so.[230] The goal of Christians should be to gain the "full knowledge" (επιγνωσις) of God's will (Colossians 1:9-10).

God works within believers, energizing their thought processes, even to the point of willing His will in them (Philippians 2:13). This involves the "tearing down" of human reason and philosophy (II Corinthians 10:5), the renewing of Christian minds (Romans 12:2), and the individual leading of the Holy Spirit (Romans 8:14). With these influences active within him, the Christian can test and find out what God's will is (Romans 12:2).

It has been established that believers have the opportunity to *know* the will of God; it is also clear that God has provided the means for them to *do* the will of God. Part of the "shepherding" work of Christ is to make believers complete for God's will, and God does His will through the believer (Hebrews 13:21). God energizes the production of His will (Philippians 2:13), making achievement possible. That accomplishment should not come from an external motivation on the Christian's part, but should come from the ψυχη, acknowledging servitude to Christ (Ephesians 6:6-7). Peace, which gives man assurance of God's will, originates in the innermost part of a believer and actually functions as an

---

[230] This is also supported by James 4:13-17, where individuals are chided for planning their own lives without consulting God's will. They "ought" to consider God's plan, and when they fail to do what they know they "ought" to do, it is sin.

arbitrator in the decisions of life (Colossians 3:15). The end result is security and confidence in decision making for the mature Christian. Those who meet the spiritual prerequisites (mentioned in the context of nearly every passage about individual guidance) can make decisions, knowing that they have discerned the will of God. Then God will help them accomplish His will.

Chapter 5

An Illustration of Specific Guidance

Once the exegesis of key passages in both Testaments has been considered, it is helpful to study a significant illustration of those principles in the Scripture. It is always important to keep in mind, however, that the doctrine of individual guidance is not based upon illustrations, but rather that the illustrations are based upon the facts of exegesis.[231]

The Search for a Wife

One of the biggest decisions that a man is ever called upon to make is the finding of a life's partner. Outside of one's own salvation, it may be the most important decision he ever faces. Obviously, this is the type of choice in which one cannot afford to make a mistake, due to the Scriptural implications of the marriage vows.[232] Since man cannot see the future, this is the kind of decision in which he should depend upon the foreknowledge of God.

---

[231] This realization helps the Bible student to avoid the danger of misinterpreting or misapplying Bible events. It is always necessary to see them in their cultural and dispensational contexts. That will help to determine if the experiences are normative or not.

[232] I Corinthians 7:39 says that the marriage vows are binding upon the believer for the life of his spouse.

The Setting

Abraham wanted a wife for his son Isaac. It was the custom for marriages to be arranged by parents or their representatives, so he felt the obligation to find just the right wife for Isaac. He delegated this responsibility to a trusted servant,[233] who set out to perform the duty, as recorded in Genesis 24.

His task was to choose one particular woman out of all the multitudes living at that time. Since there were also Messianic implications to the selection,[234] this choice was doubly important. It could not be made on the basis of physical attraction, since Isaac would not even see his bride before the arrangements were made. Neither could it be made upon the long-term observation of her character, since the servant did not already know the one he was to find. Clearly, more than human wisdom was needed. Even when there has been a long-term acquaintance and a decided physical attraction, as in most marriages in modern Western culture, the decision to take a partner for life still demands special direction from God.

---

[233] Many commentators assume this to be the Eliezer of Damascus mentioned in Genesis 15:2.
[234] Isaac was in the lineage of the promised Messiah (Genesis 17:19; Luke 3:34).

The Assurance

In the process of making this decision, the key individuals gave evidence that they knew God had directed the circumstances and led them to a decision. This was true of both the principals in the bargaining process, Abraham's servant and Laban (Rebekah's brother).

The servant's assurance. There are several statements which indicate this was a decision made with the assurance of God's direction. For instance, the servant knew that God had "appointed" a wife for Isaac and wanted to discern exactly who she was (verse 14). The word "appointed" is from יכח, meaning ". . . education and discipline as a result of God's judicial actions."[235] The use of this term demonstrates that the servant fully knew that God had already made a judgment concerning the matter.

He further implied this in verse 14 by saying that, through the meeting of certain stipulations, he would "know" (ידע) that God had answered. This word is a Qal imperfect form, which speaks of recognition and discernment."[236] The usage of this term signifies that the servant could discern the

---

[235] TWOT, s. v. "יכח," by Paul R. Gilchrist, vol. 1, 377.
[236] Ibid., s. v. "ידע," by Jack P. Lewis, 366.

truth, and that such discernment would give assurance that God was the Author of it. Twice in the chapter, the servant acknowledged that God had "led" him (verses 27, 48). In both places he used a form of נחה, which refers to ". . . the conducting of one along the right path. . . . The root is sometimes synonymous with *nahag* 'to herd' to a predetermined destination."[237]

The servant's assurance is seen in verse 48, which reveals that he knew God had led him in the "right" way. The adjective is אמת, of which has been said: "This word carries underlying sense of certainty, dependability."[238] Abraham's servant also expressed assurance regarding the decision he made by using the verb הצליח ("prospered"), in verse 56. This is a Hiphil form of צלח, signifying ". . . to make successful, to prosper."[239] The idea of this root is ". . . to accomplish satisfactorily what is intended."[240]

<u>Laban's assurance</u>. Abraham's servant was not the only one to experience the security of knowing that the decision

---

[237] Ibid., s. v. "נחה," by Leonard J. Coppes, vol. 2, 568.

[238] Ibid., s. v. "אמת," by Jack B. Smith, vol. 1, 52.

[239] Tregelles, 710.

[240] <u>TWOT</u>, s. v. "צלח," by John E. Hartley, vol. 2, 766.

was from God. Laban, the elder brother of Rebekah, who was acting head of the household, also knew that God was in it. The first indication given of Laban's assurance is in verse 50. There he declared, with the agreement of one named Bethuel,[241] that the marriage ". . . proceedeth from the Lord." The verb he used was יצא, of which the following has been observed:

> The basic notion (of this word) is "to go out." Sometimes . . . with a special emphasis on source or origin, particularly when that source is the Lord himself, as of . . . providential guidance (Gen 24:50).[242]

Still further evidence that Laban recognized the fact of God's guidance in the matter is his statement in verse 51 that the servant should take Rebekah, ", , , as the Lord hath spoken." There is no evidence that God spoke with an audible voice, but Laban knew that God had made His will known. The verb דבר is a common word, all forms of which ". . . have some

---

[241] Laban's father was named Bethuel, but Adam Clarke says this is a younger brother of Laban with the same name, assuming that the father was dead. This would require that Laban be the spokesman.
[242] TWOT, s. v. "יצא," by Paul R. Gilchrist, vol. 1, 393–394.

sense of thought processes, of communication, or of subjects or means of communication."[243]

The Prerequisites

Submissive spirit. Abraham's servant fulfilled some clear spiritual prerequisites before he came to a firm conclusion concerning Rebekah. In the first place, he had a submissive spirit toward his master and the Word of Jehovah. Abraham made him vow to refrain from considering the nearby Canaanite women, even though this required an arduous journey to the land of Mesopotamia (verses 3-4). The promise from God of a seed was to be depended upon (verse 7), and the servant sat out to obey the principles of this promise.

Prayer. Second, he made the decision a matter of prayer (verses 12-14). Adam Clarke says the reason for this prayer is that such a task required special direction from God. His assertion is that ". . . there are numberless cases, of infinite consequence to man, where his strength and prudence can be

_____

[243] Ibid., s. v. "דבר," by Earl S. Kalland, vol. 1, 179.

of little or no avail."[244] Man's weakness requires God's power and wisdom.

Godly walk. Third, he consistently walked in such a way that God could lead him. Verse 27 is his testimony: "I being in the way, the Lord led me." The "way" is the frequently-cited דֶּרֶךְ, which refers to a path worn by constant walking. It is here used metaphorically for the actions and behavior of men.[245]

Thankfulness. The fourth indication that the servant fulfilled the spiritual prerequisites was that he repeatedly "worshipped" God and credited Him with the achievement (verses 26-27, 35, 48, 52, 56). This worship was his way of expressing ". . . deep thankfulness for the guidance of the Lord."[246] Thus, the revelation of the will of God came to an individual who was walking in fellowship with his Lord, and he was aware that God was responsible for the choice.

---

[244] Adam Clarke, Genesis to Deuteronomy, vol. 1 of The Old Testament, 147.

[245] Ibid., 197-198.

[246] H. D. M. Spence and Joseph S. Exell, Genesis—Exodus, vol. 1 of The Pulpit Commentary, 303.

Non-determinative

Servant's choice. There are clear evidences that this was the non-determinative will of God. First, the servant had to make a decision (verse 4). There would be no decision for him at all if this were the determinative will of God. That which God sovereignly chooses to accomplish will be done, without dependence upon man's decision making. The *fact* of Isaac's marriage was determined by God, as evidenced by the promise of a seed, but the *person* of Isaac's marriage was non-determinative, which necessitated a choice.

Rebekah's choice. A second evidence that this is the non-determinative will of God is that the woman had a choice in the matter. This is seen from verses 5,8,39, and 58. Both Abraham and his servant acknowledged that the woman might not be "willing" (תאבה). This is a Qal imperative, third person singular, feminine verb from אבה. The root word literally means, ". . . to breathe after," and eventually came to imply ". . . to be inclined, willing, to desire."[247] In verse 58, Laban and his mother both asked Rebekah if she was willing to go, and she

---

[247] Tregelles, 4.

answered affirmatively. Both verbs are from יָלַךְ, "to go, to walk,"[248] and have future significance in this context.

Freedom and sovereignty. A third consideration that demonstrates the non-determinative nature of this situation is the statement by Abraham that the servant would bear no penalty if the woman were to refuse to cooperate (verse 8). From the servant's standpoint, he had a decision to make and was seeking guidance. From Rebekah's standpoint, she exercised volition to find happiness. In actuality, ". . . the same Divine purpose which directed the servant's way moved the heart of the damsel."[249]

The Procedural Steps

There were nine basic steps that the servant took to discern the will of God. As they are listed in the Scriptural order of the chronology, principles can be discerned that will provide a pattern for knowing the will of God in other decisions.

Began with separation . The starting point in his search for a wife for Isaac was that the servant practiced separation

---

248 Ibid., 349.
249 Spence and Exell, 299.

from the world. In verse 3 Abraham instructed him not to take a Canaanite wife, though the Canaanites offered the convenience of living in the vicinity. There was a spiritual purpose for this restriction. The Canaanite civilization was pagan and would be a compromising influence spiritually. Separation was necessary because of the ". . . growing licentiousness of the Canaanites"[250] and their idolatry, which Abraham rightly feared would detract from the worship of Jehovah.

Depended upon God's Word. The entire journey was based upon the promise that God would keep His Word. Verse 7 is Abraham's quotation of the promise of God in Genesis 17:7. This exhibited Abraham's knowledge that the individual will of God would never contradict the general will of God. That is, God will never give personal direction that conflicts with what He has already spoken. Even the use of a guiding "angel" in verse 7 (מלאכו = "messenger")[251] did not supercede the importance of the Word, but simply supplemented it.[252]

---

[250] Ibid., 297.
[251] Tregelles, 475.
[252] There is no other mention of the angel's ministry in this story. He evidently was invisible and did not speak audibly. He was doubtless active in the transaction, but none of the principals in the negotiations

Worked while he waited. One principle that is helpful in discerning the will of God is that the individual who is seeking guidance should work while he waits. That is, there is no virtue in the idea that life stops until some special direction comes from God. Verse 10 gives the simple information that the servant took ten camels and departed for Mesopotamia. Of this land it has been said that:

> . . . the name applied in particular to the area between the Tigris and Euphrates rivers, a region which in the Hebrew is called Aram, Aram-Naharaim, or Padan-Aram, along with various other names. . . In present day application the term is used of a territory practically coextensive with modern Iraq.[253]

Packing ten camels and putting together an entourage for such a difficult journey amounted to a lofty undertaking for the servant. He took with him "all his master's goods," which is doubtless a reference to a large dowry that would be given for the bride.[254] The will of God is not a haven for the lazy who sit

---

seem to be aware of his presence. It is certainly possible that God uses spirit beings to implement His will in the lives of believers, but if so, believers are unaware of their presence.

[253] Merrill C. Tenney, Pictorial Bible Dictionary, 527.
[254] Clarke, 147.

idly by waiting for special direction. Finding the will of God involves the diligence of serving God in that which has already been revealed. It seems unfair to expect God to give new instructions about what to do in the future, if one is not doing that which God has instructed for the present.

Prayed about it. A fourth step taken by the servant on his journey was that of praying specifically about the need for guidance. It is certainly appropriate to ask for God's direction in the process of making decisions. This is one way to avoid leaning on one's own understanding, while acknowledging God in all one's ways. Abraham's servant seemed to understand ". . . the danger of taking any (major) step in life without Divine guidance or instruction."[255] John's Gospel teaches us that ". . . if any man be a worshipper of God, and doeth his will, him he heareth (John 9:31b)." Romans 8:26 gives great encouragement about prayer:

> Likewise the Spirit also helpeth our infirmities: for we know not what we should pray for as we ought: but the Spirit itself maketh intercession for us with groanings which cannot be uttered.

---

[255] Spence and Exell, 299.

Prayer for wisdom is commanded in James 1:5, and there God is spoken of as giving it liberally to all men. James strongly states that it is wrong for man to plan his own time schedule, location, finances, and future without considering the will of God (James 3:13-17).

The test of circumstances. The next step that the servant took, as recorded in verse 14, is the most controversial part of the story. There he sought direction from God by praying that the woman of His choice would not only draw water for the servant, but also for the camels.

There is a controversy about whether this is an acceptable way to seek the will of God in decisions today. Friesen says that it is not, because (1) not every believer is to be married, (2) Isaac was the special promised seed of Abraham, and (3) the mention of angelic guidance in verse 7.[256] Pink, however, disagrees:

> Because the Bible is a living book no portion of it is *obsolete*, and though much that is recorded in it is ancient, yet none of it is *antiquated*. Because the Bible is a living book, every portion of it has some message

---

[256] Friesen, 299-300.

which is applicable and appropriate to our times. Because God changes not, His ways of old are, fundamentally, His ways today. Hence, God's dealings with Abraham, in the general, foreshadow His dealings with us.[257]

Actually, the servant's bargain with God was simply a way of testing the direction of God through circumstances. This is not an invalid way to carry on the process of discerning God's will. While it is acknowledged that not every believer should be married, that fact alone does not negate the principle of asking God to use circumstances to reveal His will. Some may even legitimately use circumstances to help determine whether or not to be married at all. Others may do as this servant did and use circumstances as indicators of whom to choose.

While it is granted that immature believers have abused this idea to avoid the process of diligent searching of the Scriptures and agonizing prayer, the error of some does not

---

[257] Arthur W. Pink, <u>Gleanings in Genesis</u>, vol. 1, 198-199.

make the principle wrong.[258] Some qualifications of this approach must be made, however.

It was unusual. What the servant asked for, as a sign from God, was not the normally-anticipated response. It would be an unusual woman, indeed, who would not only show hospitality to a stranger, but go far beyond Eastern courtesy to the extent of drawing water for all ten thirsty camels. The legendary ability of camels to drink large quantities after a long journey was doubtless known to the girl. Thus, the servant was asking that she give an unusual response to his request. For example, had the servant simply prayed that if the sun came up in the morning he would choose a dark-haired girl, he would not have given God much space to provide special guidance, for that would not have been unusual in Ur of the Chaldees. In order for the test of circumstances to be helpful, it must be unusual.

It was practical. There was a practical value to the request that the servant made. Since he would not have the opportunity to observe the girl's character over a long period of

---

[258] God Himself said that man's unbelief will not make God's faith "without effect" (Romans 3:3-4). It seems fair to conclude that man's abuse does not nullify God's principles.

time, he requested something that only one of exceptional character would fulfill. Matthew Henry said:

> When he came to seek a wife for his master, he did not go to the playhouse or the park, and pray that he might find one there, but to *the well of water*, expecting to find one there well employed.[259]

Thus, he was able to discern that she was a diligent worker, a woman given to hospitality, and the possessor of an energetic, unselfish spirit. To learn all of that about a woman so quickly was certainly of great practical value.

It was inconclusive. The final decision was not made solely upon the basis of the answered prayer regarding the circumstances. The servant did not immediately begin a celebration and end the search. He merely took this circumstance as one indicator, among others, that Rebekah was the right woman for Isaac. That truth points to the sixth step the servant took.

Refused to act hastily. After such a specific prayer and a correspondingly specific answer, one might expect that the

---

[259] Leslie F. Church, ed., Commentary on the Whole Bible by Matthew Henry, 42.

servant would draw his final conclusion at this point. However, such was not the case. Verse 21 says that ". . . the man wondering at her held his peace, to wit whether the Lord had made his journey prosperous or not." The phrase, "held his peace" is מחריש. This is a Hiphil participle, from חרש. This has the idea of keeping silence, or acting as if dumb.[260] The word translated, "to wit," is לדעת, an infinitive construct from ידע. Gesenius says this corresponds to οιδα in the New Testament, with the connotation of seeing, perceiving, or knowing.[261] Clearly, the servant was cautious in making his decision. He did not speak, because he was still waiting to *know* if God had prospered his journey or not.

It is important for all who use the test of circumstances to avoid the temptation of jumping to conclusions. The mere fact that an event takes place does not necessarily mean that God has arranged it in answer to the prayer of a saint. A requested circumstance may be a valid pointer toward God's will, but the entire decision should not be made on that basis alone. There is a danger in man telling God the *only* way God can reveal His will is through circumstances imagined by man.

---

[260] Tregelles, 309.
[261] Ibid., 333.

Glorified God. Although not necessarily a part of the actual process of discerning God's will, it is important that praise to God be practiced repeatedly during the entire search. In Genesis 24:26, Abraham's servant worshiped the Lord, in gratitude for the direction God had given. Glorifying God was consistently his pattern, as is seen from verses 27, 35, 48, and 52. He refused to take the credit for having superior wisdom of his own. He had asked God to lead him and responded by giving God the credit for doing so. The fervent prayer for guidance should be followed by fervent thanksgiving and praise.

In the way. Abraham's servant consistently walked in such a way that God could lead him. The statement in verse 27 is, "I being in the way, the Lord led me." The consideration of this passage has already been made earlier in this chapter. The conclusion was that the "way" is a path worn by constant walking. Since the usage of דרך here is metaphorical, it is a statement about his actions and behavior. In using this figure of speech, the servant simply claims to have established a consistent pattern of behavior that kept him in contact with God. The implication seems to be that any Christian who wants to establish a true and consistent walk with God can experience individual guidance. This is consistent with the spiritual prerequisites to guidance that were noted in so many other passages.

<u>Refused to be distracted</u>. The final principle followed by the servant in finding a bride for Isaac was that he refused to become side-tracked in his search. He had a mission to accomplish, and he wanted to be sure that he finished the task faithfully. Although he no doubt had many personal needs resulting from the long journey, his primary focus was upon the wedding arrangements. In verse 33, he refused to eat until he told his "errand."

In verses 55-56, Rebekah's family suggested that she stay home for a few days (at least ten) before traveling to marry Isaac. The servant's response was, "Hinder me not, seeing the Lord hath prospered my way." The word translated "hinder" is from אחר, meaning "delay."[262] The culmination of the business in which God had directed him was so important that the physical concerns had to be relegated to secondary importance. For the Christian, this arrangement of priorities seems to emphasize the importance of knowing and doing the will of God. The security that comes with knowing God's will also brings an urgency to the task.

---

[262] TWOT, s. v. "אחר," by R. Laird Harris, vol. 1, 33.

Friesen has said that the events of Genesis 24 are not normative for men today.[263] That is granted, if he uses "normative" to mean that all believers must use a system like this all of the time. Rather, it seems that this is an *optional* practice in discerning God's will. This option should be available to be used in connection with other indicators of the will of God, such as circumstances, counsel, and inner peace.

Applicability for Today

No study of Genesis 24 is complete without a consideration of how it applies to life today. Certainly, the events took place in another dispensation, preceding even the writing of the Pentateuch. Thus, it is important to see what effect a dispensational change has upon the individual's experience.

Dispensational Changes

Dispensational theology is an attempt to provide a proper view of history, a proper concept of progress, a proper goal for human history, and a proper unifying principle in Bible study.[264] It is an acknowledgement that God's

---

[263] Friesen, 299-300.
[264] Ryrie, 20.

expectations for mankind have been refined as His revelations to man have increased. The aspect of the matter which concerns this study is the extent of the changes that take place when new dispensations come into being.

Some things unchanged. When a new dispensation comes into being, it is not necessarily true that everything must change. Sauer says that a distinction should be maintained between direct interpretation, which does *not* always apply when a dispensation changes, and indirect practical application, which *does* always apply.[265] It is his assertion that three things accompany a dispensational change: (1) certain valid ordinances continue, (2) certain ordinances are nullified, and (3) certain new principles are introduced.[266]

This study is based upon the premise that individual guidance for believers is a practice that continues throughout the dispensations. The Dispensation of Promise, which was in effect when the events of Genesis 24 took place, was replaced by that of the Mosaiac Law, but instructions for guidance were given to the Age of Law in the Psalms and Proverbs. The Local

---

[265] Erich Sauer, The Dawn of World Redemption, 195.
[266] Ibid., 194.

Church Age followed, with still further instruction concerning guidance in the Epistles.

Unity of the Testaments. It has been said that ". . . the New Testament is the key to the proper interpretation of the Old."[267] If Old Testament practices are fulfilled or replaced, they are not to be binding upon believers in the present age. The two Testaments are not in conflict with each other, but are complementary. The pictures in the Old find fulfillment in the New. This unity has been overlooked by some dispensationalists, according to Ryrie,[268] but it should be emphasized. Even his notation of the distinctions in different dispensations makes allowance for the intended unity of the Scriptures:

> Thus the distinguishing characteristics of a different dispensation are: (1) a change in God's governmental relationship with man (though a dispensation does not have to be composed entirely of completely new features), (2) a resultant change in man's responsibility,

---

[267] John Jefferson Davis, Foundations of Evangelical Theology, 257.
[268] Ryrie, 37-38.

and (3) corresponding revelations necessary to effect the change. . . . [269]

Individual Experiences

Having seen that the matter of individual guidance is not negated by dispensational changes, the Bible student must determine if there are theological reasons to reject the idea of God's inner working in his heart today. Vos seems to give credence to individual experiences by asserting that, "God reveals Himself to the inner sense of man through the religious consciousness and the moral conscience."[270] The subjectivity of those experiences is not necessarily wrong, for even the canonization of the Word of God was not a totally objective process.

> The church's reception of the canon was due to a combination of objective factors (authorship, orthodox content) and subjective factors (Spirit's witness to the believing church), overruled and superintended by the sovereign providence of God.[271]

---

[269] Ibid., 37-38.
[270] Geerhardus Vos, Biblical Theology, 28.
[271] Davis, 200.

<u>Vitality of experience</u>. Since the very acceptance of God's Word has a partially-subjective basis, a new appreciation can be held for God's inner working. Davis says that there can be no living New Testament faith without the vitality of experience,[272] and that ". . . our religious experience is not the norm of truth, but it is the medium or channel through which that truth becomes real and personal to us."[273] He further states:

> While many church members today are suspicious of all "enthusiasm" and emotionalism in religion, it is undeniable that in both testaments God touches the whole person, including the emotions. A religion without "holy affections" in the proper sense is not the religion of the Bible, but some pale and atrophied imitation of it.[274]

<u>Warning</u>. Advocating the legitimacy of inner direction from God should be accompanied by a warning concerning the inherent dangers of such a position. The ecstatic experience of the Charismatic view can be very subjectively impressive, but if

---

[272] Ibid., 166.
[273] Ibid., 167.
[274] Ibid., 148.

the results are infidelity to the written Word of God, they must be rejected.[275] It should be remembered that:

> Not all "intuitions, impulses, leadings" are from God. The world, the flesh, and the devil, as well as the God of the Bible, can speak through our inward subjectivity. Without the normative and rationally comprehensible doctrines of scripture we are left defenseless against the seductions of alien spirits, ideologies, and forces.[276]

It becomes important, then, to check out all inner feelings in light of the clear teaching of God's Word. Howard says that the guidelines for evaluating inner desires can be condensed into three statements. Essentially, he says that God's will can never contradict the written Word, will not usually contradict common sense, nor will it usually contradict circumstantial evidence and Godly counsel.[277] Agreement is seen in the following statement by M. Blaine Smith:

> In any case, if we suspect God is trying to convey a special message to us through our intuition, we have the right (and really the responsibility) to check this out

---

[275] Ibid., 162.
[276] Ibid., 158.
[277] Howard, 87.

through other means. . . . Taking precautions with intuition should not be thought of as a lack of faith, but as our responsibility to guard against error.[278]

Heeding these repeated warnings should help the sincere believer avoid the errors of the immature.[279] Immature Christians not only misrepresent the circumstances and inner guidance occasionally, but they often misinterpret the Bible as well. There is no kind of individual direction, not even that of an angel from heaven (Galatians 1:8), that can properly contradict what God has already stated in His Word.

Conclusion

Since there is no Bible teaching against individual direction, nor any indication that it is dispensationally or theologically wrong, it is unfair to reject the idea of personal guidance on those bases. Added to the fact that there are numerous passages in the Word that speak of such guidance (several of which have been considered in previous sections of this study), it seems a proper conclusion that believers today should seek for inward direction from God. And in seeking

---

[278] Smith, 81.
[279] Friesen, 123.

such guidance, all indicators of direction must stand the test of allegiance to the Bible. Spiritual immaturity must not be allowed to misinterpret either the Bible, circumstances, Godly counsel, or inner impressions.

Chapter 6

When God Says, "No."

One of the ways that God has specifically led His people throughout Bible history is by saying, "No" to man's thoughts, desires, or actions. An investigation of some of these historical situations will provide helpful insight into the fact of just how specific the will of God is for individuals.

Sometimes it means "Never."

Of course, there are times when the "No" from God means that man should *never* be involved in a given activity. The command in Exodus 20:14, which prohibits adultery, is one of many such examples. This, of course, is the *general* will of God for all, but is included here to illustrate that "No" from God sometimes means, "Never."

Sometimes it means "Not this."

When it comes to individual guidance, however, God's "No" does not always apply to every individual and every situation. In I Chronicles 28:2-6, the record is given of David's desire to build the Temple. There was certainly nothing wrong with wanting the house of God to be built, but that was not the specific ministry God had in mind for David. God wanted David to provide substantial funds for the project, but the actual construction was not what God wanted David to do.

That job was specifically given to Solomon (verse 6). Construction of the Temple was not the specific will of God for David's ministry. God alone is qualified to determine the specific ministry that each Christian should have. It is not up to the believer to make such decisions apart from God's clear guidance. While every Christian should serve God in some manner, the individual believer must not make his own independent decision of what that service should involve. God has every right to direct each believer to fill the "niche" for which God made him, particularly since he will not fit into any other "niche."

Sometimes it means "Not now."

The story of David desiring to fight the Philistines in the Valley of Rephaim is recorded in II Samuel 5:18-25. After one successful attack by God's direction (verses 19-20), David contemplated a second battle (verses 22-23), but this time, God said, "No." This answer from God meant, "not now." God wanted David to wait until just the right *time* to attack. The fact is, good things can be done at wrong times. In God's specific plan, David waited until the proper time, and another victory was accomplished (verses 23-25). God alone is qualified to determine each believer's time schedule. Even in doing a good thing, the Christian must not take "shortcuts" of his own devising. The decision to marry, for example, should also include God's *timing* as a major consideration. The importance of God's timing is also significant in the various aspects of the ministry.

Sometimes it means "Not here."

Acts 16:6-10 has already been considered in chapter four of this book, but the passage certainly is instructive at this point as well. There Paul indicated his own desire to minister in Asia and Bithynia, but somehow, God told him, "No." While Christians have been given responsibility to take the Gospel *everywhere in the world*, as part of the general will of God, no one individual could accomplish this all by himself. Thus, it appears that God has in mind the specific *place* He wants each believer to go. The specific place God wanted for Paul to minister at that time was in Macedonia, and Paul became convinced that God had "called" him to do so (verse 10). God alone is qualified to choose the location where each believer should serve Him. A prospective missionary should not merely "throw a dart at a map," and decide on that basis where he should minister.

Sometimes it means "Not him."

The selection and anointing of a successor to King Saul was undertaken by Samuel, and his experience in that regard is recorded in I Samuel 16:6-12. Samuel, and no doubt Jesse, thought that Eliab would be the one to anoint (verse 6), but God said, "No," in verse 7. The same was true of Abinadab (verse 8), Shammah (verse 9), and David's other four brothers (verse 10).[280] Apparently, Jesse would never have guessed that David was the one of God's choice, because David was not even present for consideration (verse 11). God, on the other hand, said, "Not him" about each of David's brothers. Just as Solomon was later selected to build the Temple, David was here chosen to be Israel's next king (verse 12). God chooses individuals for specific ministries and roles, and He alone is qualified to decide who does what in His service. Believers must not depend upon their own understanding of things, in selecting individuals for leadership or service positions (Proverbs 3:5-6).

God often leads by stopping man from making mistakes. In the examples listed above, utilizing both the Old and New Testaments, it becomes abundantly clear that God has a specific, detailed will for individual believers that includes the proper activities, timing, location, and personnel for his service.

---

[280] According to I Samuel 17:12, Jesse had eight sons (including David), so in chapter 16, the other seven passed before Samuel while David was still out in the field. Six of the seven older brothers, along with David, are named in I Chronicles 2:13-15.

Chapter 7

General Application Principles

The exegesis of key passages in both Testaments has been considered, and a Biblical illustration of guidance has been noted. Now some principles of application should be seen, in order to put the system of decision making into a Biblical and practical perspective.

The Challenge of James 4:17

An often-quoted passage of Scripture is James 4:17: "Therefore to him that knoweth to do good, and doeth it not, to him it is sin." This has been applied to all types of sins of omission, including the failure to tithe, witness, attend church services, and so forth. While these all may be valid as secondary applications since commandments to do them are found elsewhere in Scripture, the primary application must be understood on the basis of the preceding context.

The Context

The paragraph in which the verse under consideration appears begins with verse 13.

> Go to now, ye that say, To day or to morrow we will go into such a city, and continue there a year, and buy and sell, and get gain: whereas ye know not what shall

be on the morrow. For what is your life? It is even a vapour, that appeareth for a little time, and then vanisheth away. For that ye ought to say, If the Lord will, we shall live, and do this or that. But now ye rejoice in your boastings: all such rejoicing is evil. Therefore to him that knoweth to do good, and doeth it not, to him it is sin.

This passage presents an indictment against those who plan their lives presumptuously, without considering the will of God. They plan their own time schedules ("today or tomorrow. . . . continue there a year. . . . "), locations (". . . go into such a city. . . ."), vocations (". . . buy and sell. . . ."), and finances (". . . get gain."). They are leaning entirely upon their own understanding, without considering God's will for their lives. The command of verse 15 is that man ought to allow the will of God to change his plans. It is this challenge that verse 17 speaks of, when omission is referred to as sin. Failure to consider *God's* plan when making one's own, then, is clearly called "sin" (αμαρτια) in the Word of God.[281] This is to be

---

[281] Some see this as simply referring to the sovereign will of God. It is true that God has the power to alter man's plans, and no man should presumptuously deny this fact. However, the magnitude of the types of decisions exhibited here is significant. These are major decisions, which

taken so seriously that one author even expresses doubt concerning the salvation of those who live so presumptuously:

> To know God's will is the proper concern of every obedient Christian. If a person professes to be a Christian but has no sense of inner obligation to know and to do God's will, we may well question whether he truly is a child of God.[282]

Woods' judgment of James' readers is unduly harsh, in light of the fact that James calls them "brethren" in verse 11. Nevertheless, the quotation above emphasizes the importance of believers knowing and doing God's will.

Areas of Concern

The text considered here lists four main areas of concern about God's will which man must consider. They all have an implication of importance, obviously with lasting

---

should be made with particular care. In this study it will be seen that major decisions require the individual leading of God. Also, the James passage places responsibility upon man, which is more easily applied if this is seen as the *specific* will of God, rather than the *sovereign* will, which man cannot prevent from occurring. How can man "sin" by violating God's *sovereign* will?

[282] C. Stacey Woods, Some Ways of God, 39.

consequences. An individual's location, vocation, time schedule, and financial dealings all affect his testimony, ministry, and family. These are not plans to be made lightly. The individual who flippantly does so has a definite problem with pride, as verse 16 reveals.

Clarke teaches that these presumptuous boasters lived under the delusion of self-sufficiency, priding themselves in their freedom from superstition by not acknowledging the will of God.[283] Alfred Plummer calls it ". . . the arrogant trust in the security of human undertakings, without consideration of God's will."[284] The seriousness of this passage demands that believers understand the significance of certain decisions that have to be made in life. The types of decisions mentioned in James 4 require special guidance from God.

Small Decisions

Seeking special guidance has been fallaciously attacked by Friesen, using the *argumentum ad ridiculum*. He pictures Christians who use the traditional approach of decision making as inconsistent because they do not pray about which shoe to

---

[283] Clarke, Romans to the Revelations, vol. 2, 823.
[284] W. Robertson Nicoll, vol. 6, 618.

put on first in the morning or which pew to sit in at church.[285] Yet, he readily admits that these are "... small, seemingly unimportant decisions."[286] The traditional view may need some refinement in this area, because virtually no one agonizes in prayer about *every* decision made in life. There are some decisions, however, that appear to have long-range consequences, which should be given more careful consideration. No doubt, the "wisdom" method also has its own hierarchy of importance in decision making. For example, is "wisdom" required in determining which shoe to put on first? No matter which concept of the will of God one follows, it is obviously true that certain decisions require more diligence than do others.

The Relative Importance of Decisions

Traditionalists need to re-define their position regarding the relative importance of decisions. There are those who have said that all decisions should be carefully prayed over, with special direction sought from God,[287] but few people actually pray about which brand of gasoline to put in their

---

[285] Friesen, 120.
[286] Ibid.
[287] Morgan, 71-72.

automobiles, or what time to get up in the morning. While there may be unforeseen consequences to these minor decisions, that which is foreseen does not seem to warrant an undue expense of time and effort in consideration.

Foreseeable Consequences

However, there are many decisions that can be seen to have lasting effects, which require more thoughtfulness. Four examples are given in James 4:13, and others can be speculated.

Time schedules. The boasters of James 4:13 had already made their plans for "to day or to morrow" and for the following year. This, of course, is in direct contradiction of God, Who said, "Boast not thyself of to morrow; for thou knowest not what a day may bring forth (Proverbs 27:1)." James reminds us that life is just a "vapour," in verse 14. The word he used is ατμις, a "mist," "stream," or "vapor," picturing that which passes away.[288] This is God's way of reminding man that time schedules are not solely controlled by man. The uncertainty of the future demands that man surrender his time to God's plan.

---

[288] BAG, s. v. "ατμις," 120.

Location. Extremely important in God's plan for man is the *place* where man serves God. The presumptuous ones who choose their own "city" in verse 13 are not allowing God to direct and control their contacts and circles of influence. Certainly, every Christian's "Jerusalem" of ministry ought to be the choice of the omniscient God. It is there that God brings the believer into contact with those whom he could influence for Christ. Since the "steps" of a Godly man are ordered by God (Psalm 37:23), it stands to reason that the *destination* of those steps has also a Divine origin.

It is also true that the friends one makes are largely determined by location. Thus, the kind of relationships that mold character, build convictions, and help establish goals in life are greatly influenced by the location in which one finds himself.

Vocation. As the boasters of James 4:13 express their self-determination to "buy and sell," they use the Greek term εμπορευσομεθα, which is a future deponent, first person plural form of εμπορευομαι. The root means, ". . . to carry on business."[289] One author has said of the Apostle Paul:

---

[289] Ibid., s. v. "εμπορευομαι," 256.

He was an apostle "by the will of God," and he described himself as having been made a minister of the gospel (Eph 3:7). He was appointed to be a preacher, apostle, and teacher (2 Ti 1:11). It is true, of course, that he labored with his hands to support himself and his colleagues (Acts 20:34); but he did not regard tent-making as his vocation. He never referred to himself as a "tent-maker by the will of God," although certainly he did not take himself out of the will of God by resorting now and again to his old trade. He was an apostle; he made tents simply to pay the bills.[290]

Some may conclude that only the vocational pastors, missionaries, and evangelists need to know the will of God. That, of course, is simply not true. When a Christian sees his occupation as a potential ministry, he recognizes a much greater significance to the type and place of employment in which he is engaged. A plumber who is in the will of God, for example, may have opportunities to witness to other plumbers or customers who would never listen to a vocational preacher of God's Word.

---

[290] J. Herbert Kane, Understanding Christian Missions, 40.

Finances. The proud merchants of James 4 have a positive plan to prosper financially in their business dealings. They plan to "get gain" (κερδησομεν). This word is a future form of κερδαινω, which means, ". . . to make a profit."[291] The planning of one's material life and well-being without seeking the direction of God is presumptuous. Since every material possession that a believer has comes from God, rather than from his own might and cleverness,[292] it is certainly appropriate that this area of life be surrendered to the will of God also. God ought to be prayerfully consulted in financial decisions such as major purchases, whether and how much insurance to buy, retirement plans, giving to others, and much, much more. These decisions require an understanding of the future that man does not possess.

Marriage. Other than personal salvation, perhaps no decision has a greater impact on one's life than the choice of a marriage partner. A young man or young lady who uses the Bible will find some excellent principles to follow, but the

---

[291] BAG, s. v. "κερδαινω," 430.

[292] This principle is stated in God's instructions for the children of Israel during the Exodus journey, as He prepared them for the material abundance that He would provide for them in Canaan (Deuteronomy 8:10-18).

choice may still be quite complex after all applicable Scriptures are studied.

It is impossible for the individual to know what the coming years will bring, necessitating the availability of special knowledge that man's wisdom does not provide. It is far too risky to "lean" unto one's own understanding, as Proverbs 3:5 warns. The "wisdom" method is an attempt to understand the present, but it cannot possibly deal with the future.[293] Since marriage is a lifetime commitment, and since the ardent husband-wife relationship has such a dramatic effect upon one's entire lifestyle and service for God, this decision should not be risked upon the limitations of human understanding.[294]

<u>College</u>. Just as not everyone should be married, not everyone should go to college, nor graduate school, nor do

---

[293] There is no guarantee that even the present is understood, since Christians do not know how to properly pray, without Divine intervention (Romans 8:26).

[294] In practice, what is the difference between "pray for wisdom" and "pray for guidance?" Is not wisdom sought as a form of guidance? Is it not asking God to work internally, utilizing God's understanding, rather than just man's? If it is not this, then why bother asking God for it? Since the "peace" advocates do not deny the validity of wisdom, but the reverse is true, it is up to the "wisdom" school to prove their mutual exclusivity.

post-graduate work. Once the choice is made to pursue higher education, however, the decision becomes almost as complex as that of choosing a wife. After consulting Bible principles, the would-be student must choose between a number of good schools. Even if the decision is narrowed down to a Fundamentalist Bible college, there are still several from which to choose. This is greatly complicated by the fact that most major decisions of life are normally made in the first few years after high school graduation. The context in which one lives during those years, and the input in his life at that time greatly influence those decisions.

As for the matter of location, the friends that will affect much of future life are often met in college. It is quite common for a spouse to be located in that context, also. How extremely important it is that the Christian be in the right place and meet the right people!

Also, one's concepts and goals concerning life and ministry (whether vocational or not), are often profoundly influenced by the training he receives. The importance of this particular decision cannot be over-emphasized. While this ought to motivate every believer to search diligently the Scriptures and pray fervently for guidance from God, it seems that more actually fear what God has planned for them. One author has said it this way:

If man "surrenders" his will to the will of God, some seem to imply, God will ask him to do the very thing he least wants to do. Nothing could be further from the truth! God's will for man is intended for his blessing and benefit. The person who seeks to do his will finds fullness of life.[295]

Merely sovereign will? Dealing with the passage considered here (James 4:13-17), Friesen does injustice to the conclusion of verse 17 (which he does not even mention). In his treatment, he indicates that this is simply the sovereign will of God and that man must not make plans that oppose it.[296] He does, however, say that James does not condemn the idea of planning, either in short-range or long-range thinking.[297]

Without intending to oppose planning, the traditionalist may note that Friesen does not deal with all of the issues here. Friesen acknowledges the open sin of commission (the "boasting" of verse 16), but he does not mention that James also speaks of a sin of omission (failure to consider God's will)

---

[295] W. Ward Gasque, "Is Man's Purpose an Enigma?" Christianity Today, 21 (July 29, 1977): 15.
[296] Friesen, 210.
[297] Ibid., 210-211.

in verse 17.[298] If this referred only to the sovereign will of God, the statement in verse 17 would lose its sense. There is nothing positive that man can do about the determinative plan of God, except to acquiesce. And, how can this refer only to planning in opposition to the sovereign will of God when planning is done *ahead of time*, and the sovereign will of God can be known only *after the fact*, according to Jay Adams?[299] While it is not denied that the sovereign will of God can interrupt the carefully laid plans of man, there is more than just that fact to this message in James. The conclusion of this paragraph of Scripture is that it is sin for man to make major plans by leaning unto his own understanding, rather than by seeking the will of God.

The Necessity of Foreknowledge

One of the aspects of God's sovereignty is the fact of His foreknowledge. Since the Scripture notes both God's sovereigny and man's free will, a Biblical position will, of necessity, see the two as complementary, rather than contradictory. A balanced view is a temperate one, which

---

[298] In fact, Friesen refers to portions of this paragraph seven different times in his book, but never once mentions verse 17, according to the Scripture index he includes.
[299] Adams, 28.

accepts Bible statements for what they actually say, rather than for what limited human logic concludes they say.

Not determinism. An example of an imbalanced view is that taken by Boettner, who claims to see the difference between foreknowledge and foreordination.[300] In application, he leans so heavily toward determinism that the two are almost indistinguishable:

> Through the Scriptures the divine foreknowledge is ever thought of as dependent on the divine purpose, and God foreknows only because He has pre-determined. His foreknowledge is but a transcript of His will as to what shall come to pass in the future, and the course which the world takes under his providential control is but the execution of His all-embracing plan. His foreknowledge of what is yet to be, whether it be in regard to the world as a whole or in regard to the detailed life of every individual, rests upon His pre-arranged plan.[301]

---

[300] Loraine Boettner, The Reformed Doctrine of Predestination, 46.
[301] Ibid., 99.

Not causative. The view of A. H. Strong seems to improve upon this position. He states that there are no ". . . assignable grounds of knowledge" that provide a basis for the Biblical doctrine of foreknowledge.[302] In other words, rather than forcing conclusions that *appear* to be logical, the Biblical view does not try to invent answers that the Scripture does not give. Strong further states that, "Omniscience embraces the actual and the possible, but it does not embrace the contradictory and the impossible, because these are not objects of knowledge."[303]

Admitting that foreknowledge (in the following quote called "prescience") presupposes the fact of predetermination, Strong puts it in the following perspective:

> Prescience is not itself causative. It is not to be confounded with the predetermining will of God. Free actions do not take place because they are foreseen, but they are foreseen because they are to take place.[304]

Man's access to foreknowledge. Man does not have the attribute of foreknowledge, and that fact limits his capability to

---

[302] A. H. A. H. Strong, 284.
[303] Ibid., 286.
[304] Ibid.

make decisions affecting his future. This lack of knowledge of the future (Proverbs 27:1) displays the folly of man's dependence upon his own wisdom. It gives special meaning to God's promise in Isaiah 45:3 (". . . I will direct all his ways"). When God pledged to "direct," He used the Piel imperfect form of ישר. The Piel provides an intensive sense, indicating a "making straight" that frees one's path from obstacles, as was done in preparation for receiving a royal visitor.[305] Thus, the foreknowledge of God frees man's דרך ("way") from obstacles. Since man cannot provide foreknowledge of his own, he must depend upon the God Who has it to direct his future.[306]

Man's Accountability to God

An often overlooked factor regarding the individual will of God is that man is accountable to God for the details of

---

[305] TWOT, s. v. "ישר," by Donald J. Wiseman, vol. 1, 17.

[306] Advocates of the "wisdom" school should ponder the following questions: (1) Do we trust God to reveal what He desires, or (2) Does He desire *nothing* (other than the moral will)? If the first question is answered in the affirmative, the case for an individual will is solid. If the second question is affirmed, the assumption must be that God accepts the decisions of man, then works "sovereignly" to make things work out properly. This seems to almost make man sovereign over God, reversing the roles of Master and servant. It is more fitting to see man adapting to the desires of God, rather than God adapting to the desires of man.

his life. This is seen in Matthew 12:36, where it is stated that man must answer for ". . . every idle word." Luke 12:2, 8-9 predicts that nothing shall be overlooked in the judgment, while II Corinthians 5:19 speaks of the judgment of both good and bad things done in the body. The reminder of Hebrews 4:13 is that ". . . all things are naked and opened unto the eyes of him with whom we have to do." The "works" and "secrets" of men will be judged, according to Romans 2:6, 16, and the "hidden things of darkness" will be eventually brought to light (II Corinthians 4:5). All of these passages speak of the magnitude of detail involved in the judgment of believers at the βημα, the Judgment Seat of Christ.

Fair judgment. The judgment of God is according to "truth" (Romans 2:2), and is always equitable. It is important that God not only be a Justifier, but that He also be "just" (Romans 3:26). If God is going to hold man accountable for words, motives, thoughts, and "secret things, " as well as actions, then it is reasonable that God would give man clear direction about His will in all of these areas. While God may not care which shoe an individual puts on first, there are obviously many details of life for which He will hold man accountable. In order for man to be judged fairly, he must have opportunity to know what God desires of him in all those areas of judgment.

Since not all of man's decisions are spelled out in the Scripture, there must be some other way for him to know what

God desires. If the believer is left to his own wisdom in decision making, there might be justifiable accusations of God, regarding the fairness of judgment. Since there is to be a detailed judgment, there must also be a detailed will of God as the basis of that judgment. All believers must have opportunity to know that will.

God's Will for Now

When a Christian has yielded to the individual will of God, he has assurance that he is doing what God wants him to do right now. It allows him to make a commitment to that which God has convinced him to do, whether it be to marriage, ministry, or whatever. That commitment sustains him through the different, and sometimes difficult, experiences which any given situation might provide. A pastor, for example, may face difficult situations, and the assurance that God has led him to that ministry coulod help him to stay and conquer, rather than to run away. When understood properly, the will of God can result in a stability that will help the believer to demonstrate steadfast character. With that understanding as a basis, the believer must yet maintain a mindset which allows God to give new instructions for the future. That is, among those commitments that are not Scripture-defined, man must allow God to give new direction whenever He chooses.

167

Relocation

The relocation of God's servants is an interesting study in the Word of God. While many individuals made moves from one place to another for apparently wrong reasons, there are clear examples of those whom God specifically instructed to relocate. A comparison of some of these will serve to illustrate this.

Wrong reasons. There are several instances of people who relocated without having proper reasons. Lot, for example, chose Sodom for materialistic reasons (Genesis 13:10-13). He saw the well-watered plain, but not the vile immorality of Sodom. The rest of his sad story, including his daily vexation (II Peter 2:7-8) and the terrific losses he eventually experienced, reveals that the choice was wrong from the beginning.

Joseph was relocated to Egypt through the evil intentions of his brothers (Genesis 37:28). In this instance, of course, the brothers were unwitting participants in fulfilling the sovereign will of God, which had ultimate good as its purpose (Genesis 45:4-8; 50:20). Moses' flight into Midian occurred, not after a soul-searching season of prayer, but as the result of carefully pre-meditated violence (Exodus 2:12). He ran in fear, not faith (verses 14-15).

Another example of one who moved without direction from God was Elimelech (Ruth 1:1-5). He was led by physical adversity (famine), but he left the place of God's appointment, where "judges" (who were leaders in spiritual, social, judicial, political, and legislative matters)[307] were in place. He sought the "prosperity" of Moab, which was forbidden in Deuteronomy 23:3-6, so he clearly had no direction from God to go there. He and his sons died in Moab; hence, he did not see the outworking of God's sovereign plan (which included placing Ruth in he lineage of the Messiah).

In each of these cases of wrong decisions, the sovereign God overruled to accomplish something beneficial, but that does not necessarily make the human decisions proper.

God's direction. The Old Testament also gives examples of men who relocated at the command of God. Abraham, in Genesis 12:1-4, received specific instructions from God to leave his homeland. With the command came a promise of reward for obedience. The journey was such a step of faith that Abraham did not even know where he was going. It was not until he arrived in Canaan that God revealed to him the actual location (verses 6-7).

---

[307] Francis Brown, S. R. Driver, and Charles A. Briggs, eds., Hebrew and English Lexicon of the Old Testament, s. v. "שׁפט," 1047.

A second example is found in Genesis 28-29. Jacob, obeying his father's command to separate from the pagan Canaanites when looking for a wife, traveled to Padan-Aram to seek a bride (28:1-2). He trusted in the Word of God (28:3-4) and enjoyed God's presence (28:12-16). Could a serious reader of the Bible conclude that his meeting with Rachel was just a chance circumstance? It seems obvious that God directed both his steps and hers.

In Genesis 31:3 he again relocated, at the command of God. The move made by Jacob into Egypt is described in Genesis 46:2-7. There, the seed thought of moving was occasioned by the same physical adversity which Elimelech later faced. In Jacob's case, however, God personally confirmed that the move was proper (verse 3), and God promised His own presence (verse 4). God also said that He would bring Jacob back to Canaan again. Thus, it was the will of God for him to be in Canaan for awhile, in Egypt for awhile, and then back to Canaan again.

Moses, who has already been seen to be an example of an improper move, made another move in Exodus 3:10. This move was made in the will of God. God commanded the change, promised His presence (verse 12), and also promised victory (verse 18) and opposition (verse 19). Later, Moses desired to go into Canaan and begged God for the privilege (Deuteronomy 3:25). God opposed it (verse 26), but He did allow Moses to see the land (verse 27). Human wisdom and desires were negated by God. The result was that Moses could not enter Canaan (verse 29).

The entire nation of Israel, of course, was commanded by God to leave Egypt, which they did, in Exodus 12:37. They were led by the physical presence of God (40:36-38), resulting in a journey that was composed of forty-two different segments (see Numbers 33), though it could have been shortened, had they trusted God and gone into the land earlier. At the end of the Exodus, Joshua was commanded by God, through Moses, to journey into Canaan (Deuteronomy 31:23). This command also included the promise of God's presence and the promise of victory, as recorded in Joshua 1:3-5.

Yet another example is Caleb, who is described as one who "wholly followed" the Lord (Joshua 14:8). He chose a difficult task, desiring to prove God's power and presence (verse 12). He was rewarded because he "wholly followed" God (verse 14).

The final example to be considered here is that of Gideon in Judges 6. He is directly commanded by "the angel of the Lord" to go into battle against the Midianites (verse 14). He was reluctant to go, but God promised His presence and victory (verses 15-16). He accepted peace from God in the matter (verses 23-24) but still wavered, to the point of requiring verification through the signs of the fleece (verses 36-40). Even though the circumstantial evidence that Gideon

171

sought was not necessarily the demonstration of exemplary faith, it is still significant that the "fleece" did not contradict either the direct commandment of God or the inner peace that Gideon had been given. It also should be noted that God, rather than refusing Gideon's terms, brought about the confirmation he had requested.

Many other illustrations of movement can be seen in Scripture, but these describe several different circumstances, while revealing some consistent principles. While there may be a temptation to dismiss these as examples of special revelation, there is benefit to giving the matter more consideration. Dealing with the related subject of the "call" of God, Benjamin McGrew's paper speaks of direct communication from God. His conclusion is that God is *able* to give direct communication today, but His purposes do not indicate that He will.[308] Although the *means* of communication may not be the same today, that does not negate the *fact* of communication from God.

---

[308] Benjamin J. McGrew, Jr., "A Discussion of the 'Call' to the Ministry," a paper presented at Baptist Bible College and Seminary, September 21, 1982, 37.

Observations. Some concluding observations can be made from the above examples of the relocation of God's servants. One important thought is that those who made their own plans without being directed by God suffered great losses. Second, in many of the situations in which God gave clear direction, He also promised His presence and victory. Third, the real achievement of important goals came, not through the wisdom of man, but as a result of the direction from God.[309]

The last orders given. When it is acknowledged that God can change a Christian soldier's marching orders at any time, another important consideration must be made. That is, how does one know when to make a change? How can a Christian make a firm commitment to a given decision, if God might reveal new details at any time? On the other hand, how can one avoid the instability of a restless spirit? One simple idea can be helpful in this dilemma. Every believer should continue doing faithfully the last duty God revealed to Him. As new

---

[309] There were various supernatural activities accompanying God's direction to Bible characters. Sometimes an angel appeared, sometimes there were visions or dreams, sometimes physical miracles (as in the burning bush), and sometimes an audible voice was heard. However, none of these happened in *every* case, which leads one to believe that those experiences should not be considered normative. The one common experience was the communication of God's individual will.

opportunities come along, the believer must have a single purpose and steadfastly follow the last orders known to be given by God.

There should be full persuasion in the Christian's mind (Romans 14:5) before he changes his course of action. Anything less than that would be a sin (Romans 14:23). After one has come to the conclusion that God has led him to a certain position, the burden of proof ought to be on making a change. The lack of convincing from God should be interpreted as a reason to be "steadfast, unmoveable."

Overcoming hardship. This approach should help the Christian to see difficulty as an obstacle to hurdle, rather than as a stop sign. Without recognizing individual guidance, one might interpret difficulty as sufficient reason to terminate a ministry that God wanted him to continue. To avoid the tendency of immaturity to second-guess decisions, Smith gives the following advice:

> I must trust that God allowed me to have the information I needed at the time of the decision and likewise withheld information that might have discouraged me from going where he wanted. Later

information may signal a change in direction, but it cannot challenge my original understanding of God's will. God leads as much by information he withholds as by information he gives.[310]

Suggestions from Various Authors

Several individuals who have constructed schemes of discerning the will of God have given suggestions for others to consider. George Mueller, noted for the effectiveness of his faith and prayer life, followed a six-step process. First, he determined to prepare his heart to forsake its own natural willfulness. Second, he refused to decide only on the basis of feelings or impressions. Third, he sought the will of God in connection with the Word of God, making sure that the Word and the Spirit agreed. Fourth, he considered the direction given by providential circumstances. Fifth, he prayed for God to reveal His will. Sixth, after prayer, study of the Word, and reflection, he made a decision based upon the abiding peace that the Lord gave him.[311]

---

[310] Smith, 34.
[311] Basil Miller, George Mueller: Man of Faith & Miracles, 50-51.

Arnold and Tompkins suggest that, "If we are open to the internal nudgings of the Holy Spirit this decision making process is greatly enhanced."[312] The same authors state that establishing a relationship with God and working in His service as a top priority greatly simplify the decision making process for Christians. Their contention is that many debatable alternatives are eliminated by the clarity of the Bible regarding ". . . a surprising number of activities."[313]

After listing several "prerequisites" and "signposts" in the attempt to discern God's will, Nelson says that inner peace may not be a reliable indicator if those prerequisites and signposts have been neglected. They check our tendency to assume peace about things that contradict God's real desires.[314] He also advocates repetitious prayer for wisdom, citing the usage of the present tense (continual action) in James 1:5.[315] He expands on the wisdom idea in this way:

> That a man needs to be thinking along the lines of
> God's wisdom is obvious if he is going to discern God's

---

[312] John D. Arnold and Bert L. Tompkins, How to Make the Right Decisions, 6.
[313] Ibid., 6-7.
[314] Nelson, 77.
[315] Ibid., 58.

will (see Isa 55:8-9). To make a decision about a problem that is close to what God wants one must think in much the same way that God thinks. We need to be equipped with God's wisdom in order to discern and do His will.[316]

This section can be concluded with the observation of Howard, who says that the "desired" (non-determinative) will of God is discovered *primarily* in the Word of God, through precepts and principles. It is discovered *secondarily* through circumstances, counsel, consequences, conscience, common sense, compulsion, and contentment.[317]

Reasons for Doing God's Will

The reasons for doing the will of God are numerous. The suggestions of two authors will be presented here. Nelson lists the following as the Christian's motivation to do God's will:

> First, because we love Him (John 14:15, 21, 23-24) and want to please Him (I John 3:22). . . . Second, because in return for our obedience we will receive blessing in

---

[316] Ibid., 38.
[317] Howard, 125.

this life (I Peter 3:10-12) and rewards in the future life (I Corinthians 3:10-15; II Timothy 4:8; Heb 10:35). . . . Third, to avoid chastening by the Lord in this life (I Cor.3:16-17; 11:31-32; I Peter 4:17). . . . Fourth, to be a good example to other Christians (I Cor. 4:16; I Thess. 1:7; II Thess. 3:9; Heb. 13:7). . . . Fifth, because in this way we will avoid being ashamed at Christ's second coming (I John 2:28).[318]

Coder adds the following reasons for knowing God's will: we are incapable of planning our own lives (Jeremiah 10:23), only God knows the future (Isaiah 46:9-10), God wants us to know His will (Colossians 1:9), and God commands us to know and do His will (Ephesians 5:17; 6:6)[319]

Summary

James 4:13-17 teaches that it is sin for Christians to make major decisions without considering the will of God. There are many decisions which have foreseeable consequences. These require that man draw upon the foreknowledge of God, as a resource for planning the future.

---

[318] Nelson, 8.
[319] Coder, 16-23.

Major decisions must be made, for example, in the areas of location, vocation, finances, marriage, education, and ministry. The importance of making right decisions is seen in the fact that believers will face detailed judgment at the βημα.

God has the right to reveal new plans for His servants whenever He chooses. He has directed some in the past to relocate, while others apparently moved without His leadership. It is wise for the Christian to maintain current duties, until he is fully persuaded that God has given new orders. Such an approach will help to produce security and stability within the believer. It will also assist him in overcoming obstacles he faces, and to avoid "second-guessing."

Many authors give advice concerning God's will. They must all be evaluated Scripturally as the individual attempts to make Godly decisions.

Chapter 8

Pointers to the Will of God

There are several factors to be taken into account when one is seeking the individual will of God. The first and foremost factor is the written Word, which transcends all other indicators available to the believer. Then he may consider the consensus of Godly counselors, the evaluation of circumstances, Godly wisdom, and inner peace (or the *absence* of it). Throughout the process, he should pray fervently and importunately for guidance. These subjects, with their Biblical indications, will be noted here, to assist the believer in decision making.

The Word of God

The primary source for discerning the will of God is the Bible. It is a "lamp" and a "light" for the believer (Psalm 119:105). That is, the Christian's way is enlightened by the Word. Chapter two of this study has already elaborated on the need to view Biblical commands from a dispensational and cultural understanding, to know exactly how to best obey them and their underlying principles. This is the supreme pointer to the will of God. That is, none of the other pointers can legitimately contradict this one. Since it expresses God's general will for everyone, its principles are safe ground when one is making individual decisions. Once Biblical commands have been obeyed and Biblical principles taken into consideration, many decisions of life can be made with the assurance that God has directed through His Word.

Prayer

    Prayer for guidance. When desiring to know God's specific will, it is important to make the decision a matter of persistent, importunate prayer. Matthew 7:7 gives a familiar three-fold imperative, with corresponding promises: "Ask, and it shall be given you; seek, and ye shall find; knock, and it shall be opened unto you." All three of these imperatives are in the present tense, which indicates the command for *continual* asking, seeking, and knocking. While this might have many applications, it certainly is appropriate to claim this verse in decision making. Since God has already obligated Himself to provide guidance for the obedient Christian, this type of prayer is the believer's way of submitting the process to God's greater wisdom. The prayer for guidance has been seen in chapter four of this study, in the exegesis of Colossians 1:9. In that passage, Paul prayed that the Colossians would be ". . . filled with the knowledge of his will. . . ." Epaphras also prayed for the Colossians, as recorded in chapter 4, verse 12 of the same epistle: ". . . labouring fervently for you in prayers, that ye may stand perfect and complete in all the will of God." While these statements in Colossians refer to *intercessory prayer for others* to know the will of God, it stands to reason that each individual should pray for his own guidance from God.

Prayer for God's will. When a believer prays, he is not demanding of God, nor is he giving God a list of things that God *must* do for him. Prayer is probably best understood in the Medieval scenario of a subject pleading his cause before the king. When the subject "prayed" that the king would hearken, he did so with a humble, submissive spirit, acknowledging the king's authority to do whatever he pleased. In Mark 1:40, a leper said to Jesus, ". . . If thou wilt, thou canst make me clean." He did not *demand* healing, but he acknowledged Jesus' power to heal and submitted the actual healing to the will of the Master. Jesus Himself, dreading the defilement of the guilt of man's sin and the resultant loss of fellowship with the Father, prayed, "O my Father, if it be possible, let this cup pass from me: nevertheless not as I will, but as thou wilt (Matthew 26:39)." When one seeks God's face for guidance in decision making, he must not arrogantly *demand* of God, but should humbly submit to God's timetable and means of guidance.

Sometimes fasting is needed. Jesus explained to His disciples that there are some spiritual battles that require an extra level of self-denial, in Matthew 17:21. When the disciples questioned why they were unable to cast out a certain demon, Jesus answered, ". . . this kind goeth not out but by prayer and fasting." Fasting is not necessarily required in every situation, but there are some particularly significant decisions that may demand a deeper level of commitment to God. Surely, the will of God is so needful that it is a small sacrifice to temporarily deny the flesh, in order to make sure that the Spirit of God is dominant in one's life.

Seeking Counsel

It is also beneficial to receive advice from a number of Godly individuals who are experienced in serving God. While some might rely merely upon one "spiritual guru," the admonition of the Scripture is to use a ". . . multitude of counselors (Proverbs 11:14; 15:22; 24:6)." It was a number of Godly individuals who counseled Paul, through the Holy Spirit, advising him to not go to Jerusalem (Acts 21:4, 11). Such counselors ought to be spiritually mature and preferably older than the counselee, since the Bible speaks of the "hoary head" as a "crown of glory," in Proverbs 16:31. It is a shame that many young people seek counsel from their peers, most of whom have the same problems, when God has provided them with access to mature, experienced saints who could advise them.

A warning to counselors. Those who find themselves being asked for counsel should not take lightly the seriousness of advising others. The counselor should see himself as a tool in the process of discerning the will of God, rather than a "dictator" who expects counselees to agree with the counselor's every opinion. Some are all too willing to tell others whom they should marry, where they should attend college, where and how they should serve God, *etc.* Counseling is not simply an opportunity to dominate others, nor to impose one's own will on others, but is a ministry of helping the counselee to discern God's specific will for him. Perhaps counselors should restrain their tendencies toward dogmatism, and express their views as *opinions*, and *observations*, but acknowledge that the Biblical plan is for the counselee to seek a "multitude" of counselors. Some people are quick to give dogmatic advice, the consequences with which *others* would have to live!

Godly Reasoning

In James 1:5, the seeker of wisdom is told to ". . . ask of God, that giveth to all men liberally, and upbraideth not; and it shall be given him." This wisdom for which the believer should pray is simply Holy Spirit-enlightened reasoning, within the parameters of Biblical truth. It is not humanistic rationalism, but it is the highest form of logic, the kind that reasons in accordance with Scriptural principles. It evaluates the "substance" and "evidence" of faith (Hebrews 11:2). God has given man a measure of intelligence, and it should be used to produce Biblical logic. It is often useful to weigh the lists of "pros" and "cons" of a given situation, giving the greatest weight to those issues to which God attaches importance.

Circumstances

The proper evaluation of circumstances plays a part in Godly decision making. It is certainly true that the sovereign God can arrange circumstances to direct believers into His specific will. The Apostle Paul, for example, discovered that it was the will of God for him to be a short-term missionary on the island of Melita, as the result of a storm at sea and shipwreck (Acts 17:40-28:10). Melita was certainly not on the planned agenda when the ship set sail, but God rearranged the circumstances to put Paul right where He wanted him at that time. Caution should be taken that the individual not lean so heavily upon his own understanding of circumstances that he forsakes the other pointers and makes a hasty decision, but this is one legitimate means that Christians have in discerning the specific will of God.

<u>Peace</u>

Exegetical work on Colossians 3:15 has already been produced here in chapter four, but it is good to be reminded that believers should ". . . let the peace of God rule in your hearts. . . ." Once the steps of Bible study, prayer, seeking counsel, Godly reasoning, and circumstances have all been evaluated, the peace that God provides as the "arbitrator" in decisions can help to make the final decision. That is, if one has peace, he has the *assurance* that the decision is right, and he should proceed. However, if he is still uncertain, he does not have the necessary peace, and he is not yet ready to make the decision. Without peace regarding a new direction, the Christian ought to continue doing the last thing he knew that God wanted him to do. This peace is designed by God to give security and avoid "second-guessing."

Chapter 9

Conclusion

It has been the purpose of this book to demonstrate from the Scriptures that there is a specific will of God for individual believers. That specific will can be known and accomplished by those individuals.

The introductory chapter justified the study by noting that the subject of individual guidance has been challenged in a book by Garry Friesen, entitled, <u>Decision Making and the Will of God</u>. Friesen denied the existence of an individual will of God and rejected the validity of peace in one's heart as an indicator of that will. He advocated that Christians merely use applied wisdom in making decisions which are not specifically mandated by God's Word.

There are two main aspects of the will of God. The determinative, or sovereign, will is that which God will accomplish regardless of man's efforts or response. The non-determinative will is that which God wants to accomplish through man's volition.

It is agreed among Bible-believers that there is a general (moral) will of God, which is part of God's non-determinative will. This general will is found in the Bible, which gives common instructions to all believers, when interpreted culturally and dispensationally. The point of contention is seen in Friesen's challenge to the traditionally-accepted view that the non-determinative will also includes specific details for individual believers. The individual will is to be discovered through both objective and subjective sources.

There are numerous Old Testament passages that speak of individual guidance. These portions reveal that guidance was experienced in several of the dispensations, leading to the conclusion that individual guidance transcends dispensational changes.

The Old Testament teaches that individual guidance was given to saints who had met spiritual prerequisites. It came through both internal and external means, with the primary emphasis being on God's internal influence upon man. The Old Testament concept of the individual will included detailed specifics, pointing to the particulars of a Godly lifestyle.

The knowledge of such a specific plan provided security for those believers who followed, but the individual who failed to consult God was guilty of sin. The superiority of God's ways and thoughts provided wonderful benefits for those who responded tenderly to the influence that God placed upon their thinking processes.

The New Testament also includes numerous passages about individual guidance, dealing with both *knowing* and *doing* the will of God. Confirmation of the Old Testament principles of guidance is found in the New Testament, including the realization that failure to understand the will of God is sin. God is presented in the New Testament as energizing man's will toward right desires, then providing the energy for the accomplishment of those God-given desires. Assurance is given to the Christian through inner peace, which acts as an arbitrator in decision making.

An illustration of specific guidance is seen in the story of the selection of a wife for Isaac, in Genesis 24. The story includes the meeting of spiritual prerequisites, prayerful consideration of circumstances, and assurance of God's direction. Nine procedural steps were taken by Abraham's servant in decision making: (1) he began with separation from the world; (2) he depended upon God's Word; (3) he worked while he waited; (4) he prayed about it; (5) he employed a circumstantial test; (6) he refused to act hastily; (7) he repeatedly glorified God in the search; (8) he consistently lived in such a way that God could lead him; and (9) he refused to be distracted. A brief study of the validity of human experience in the Christian life justifies the use of this story as an optional pattern for believers today.

Certain applicational principles have been noted concerning the individual will of God. A key thought is that individual guidance should be sought in the major decisions, which are defined as those having foreseeable, lasting consequences. Such circumstances require access to the foreknowledge of God, since man does not know the future. This realization makes individual guidance of great importance. It was also noted that Christians will experience a detailed judgment by God, reinforcing the need of detailed guidance. The relocation of some servants of God has been observed, with the conclusion that some of these decisions were right and some were wrong.

Decision making should begin with a study of the Bible, before other indicators are considered. If questions still persist, there should be an evaluation of circumstances, the advice of a number of spiritually-minded believers, fervent prayer, Godly reason, and the internal peace that God gives.

Selected Bibliography

BOOKS

Abbott-Smith, G. A Manual Greek Lexicon of the NewTestament. New York: Charles Scribner's Sons, n.d.

A Greek-English Lexicon of the New Testament and Other Early Christian Literature. By Walter Bauer. Translated by William F. Arndt and Wilbur Gingrich, 4th rev. ed.

Allis, Oswald T. Prophecy and the Church. Philadelphia: Presbyterian and Reformed Publishing Company, 1945.

Analytical Greek Lexicon, The. Grand Rapids: Zondervan Publishing House, 1968.

Arnold, John D., and Bert L. Tompkins. How to Make the Right Decisions. Milford, MI: Mott Media, 1982.

Bancroft, Emery H. Elemental Theology. Grand Rapids: Zondervan Publishing House, 1960.

Barnes, Albert. Barnes' Notes on the New Testament. Grand Rapids: Kregel Publications, 1968.

Boettner, Loraine. The Reformed Doctrine of Predestination. Philadelphia: The Presbyterian and Reformed Publishing Company, 1965.

Church, Leslie F., ed. Commentary on the Whole Bible by Matthew Henry. Grand Rapids: Zondervan Publishing House, 1964.

Clarke, Adam. The New Testament of Our Lord and Savior Jesus Christ. 2 vols. New York: Abingdon Press,n.d. Vol. 2: Romans to the Revelations, by Adam Clarke.

_____. The Old Testament. 4 vols. New York: Abingdon Press, n.d. Vol. 1: Genesis to Deuteronomy, by Adam Clarke.

Coder, S. Maxwell. God's Will for Your Life. Chicago: Moody Press, 1946.

Cumberledge, Geoffrey. A Lexicon Abridged from Liddell and Scott's Greek-English Lexicon. Oxford: Clarendon Press, 1953.

Davidson, Benjamin. The Analytical Hebrew and Chaldee Lexicon. Peabody, MA: Hendrickson Publishers, 1986.

Davis, John Jefferson. Foundations of Evangelical Theology. Grand Rapids: Baker Book House, 1984.

Eadie, John. Commentary on the Epistle of Paul to the Colossians. Originally published by Richard Griffin & Co., 1856; reprint, Minneapolis: James and Klock Publishing Co., 1977.

Ellinwood, C. M. and M. J. His Will. Chicago: Published by the authors, 1907.

Friesen, Garry. Decision making and the Will of God: A Biblical Alternative to the Traditional View. Portland: Multnomah Press, 1980.

Greene, Oliver B. The Epistles of Paul the Apostle to the Colossians. Greenville, SC: The Gospel Hour, Inc., 1963.

He Kaine Diatheke (The Greek Text Underlying the English Authorized Version of 1611). London: Trinitarian Bible Society, n.d.

Hebrew Bible, The. Tulsa: Published by Oral Roberts, 1960.

Hendriksen, William. Exposition of Colossians and Philemon. Grand Rapids: Baker Book House, 1964.

_____. Exposition of Philippians. Grand Rapids: Baker Book House, 1962.

Howard, J. Grant. Knowing God's Will and Doing It! Grand Rapids: Zondervan Publishing House, 1976.

Jennings, F. C. Studies in Isaiah. New York: Loizeaux Brothers, 1950.

Kaiser, Walter C., Jr. Towards an Old Testament Theology. Grand Rapids: Zondervan Publishing House, 1978.

Kane, J. Herbert. Understanding Christian Missions. Grand Rapids: Baker Book House, 1974.

Mackay, W. P. Abundant Grace. London: Pickering & Inglis, n.d.

Meyer, F. B. The Secret of Guidance. Chicago: Moody Press, n.d.

Miller, Basil. George Mueller: Man of Faith & Miracles. Grand Rapids: Zondervan Publishing House, 1941.

Morgan, G. Campbell. God's Perfect Will. Grand Rapids: Baker Book House, 1973.

Nelson, Marion H. How to Know God's Will. Chicago: Moody Press, 1963.

Nicoll, W. Robertson, ed. The Expositor's Bible. 6 vols. Grand Rapids: William B. Eerdmans Publishing Company, 1956.

Pentecost, J. Dwight. Things to Come. Grand Rapids: Dunham Publishing Company, 1958.

Pfeiffer, Charles F., and Everett F. Harrison, eds. The Wycliffe Bible Commentary. Chicago: Moody Press, 1962.

Pierson, A. T. God's Living Oracles. London: James Nisbet and Co., Limited, 1908.

Pink, A. W. The Divine Covenants. Grand Rapids: Baker Book House, 1973.

Robertson, Archibald Thomas. Word Pictures in the New Testament. 6 vols. Nashville: Broadman Press, 1931-32. Vol. 4 (1932): The Epistles of Paul. Vol. 5 (1932): The Fourth Gospel-- The Epistle to the Hebrews, by Archibald Thomas Robertson.

Ryrie, Charles Caldwell. Dispensationalism Today. Chicago: Moody Press, 1965.

Sauer, Erich. The Dawn of World Redemption. Grand Rapids: William B. Eerdmans Publishing Company, 1952.

Scroggie, W. Graham. The Psalms. Westwood, NJ: Fleming H. Revell, 1965.

Smith, M. Blaine. Knowing God's Will. Downers Grove, IL: Intervarsity Press, 1979.

Spence, H. D. M., and Joseph S. Exell, eds. The Pulpit Commentary. 23 vols. Grand Rapids: William B. Eerdmans Publishing Company, 1975.

Spurgeon, Charles Haddon. The Treasury of David. 7 vols. New York: Funk and Wagnalls, n.d. Vol. 2: Psalm XXVII to LII; Vol. 7: Psalm CXXV to CL, by Charles H. Spurgeon.

Strong, Augustus Hopkins.Systematic Theology. Three volumes in one. Westwood, NJ: Fleming H. Revell Company, 1907.

Strong, James. The Exhaustive Concordance of the Bible. Grand Rapids: Baker Book House, n.d.

Tenney, Merrill C., ed. Pictorial Bible Dictionary. Nashville: The Southwestern Company, 1976.

The Holy Bible, New International Version. New York: International Bible Society, 1978.

Theological Dictionary of the New Testament. Edited by Gerhard Kittel and Gerhard Friedrich. Translated and edited by Geoffrey W. Bromiley. 1964-74. S.v. "ἄφρων, ἀφρόνος," by Rudolf Bultmann, 9 (1974):230-231. S.v. "βραβεύω," by Ethelbert Stauffer, 1 (1964):637-638. S.v. "γινώσκω," by Rudolf Bultmann, 1 (1964):689-714. S.v. "δόκιμος," by Walter Grundmann, 2 (1964):255-260. S.v. "δύναμαι/δύναμις," by Walter Grundmann, 2 (1964):285-317. S.v. "λατρεία," by H. Strathmann,4 (1967):65. S.v. "πληροφορέω," by Gerhard Delling,6 (1968):309-310. S.v. "πληρόω," by Gerhard Delling,6 (1968):290-298. S.v. "τέλειος," by Gerhard Delling,8 (1972):73-78.

Theological Wordbook of the Old Testament. Edited by R. Laird Harris, Gleason L. Archer, and Bruce K. Waltke. 1980. S.v.

"אחר," by R. Laird Harris, 1:33-34. S.v. "אמן," by Jack B. Scott, 1:51-53. S.v. "ארה," by Victor P. Hamilton, 1:71. S.v. "דרך," by Herbert Wolf, 1:196-197. S.v. "ידע," by Paul R. Gilchrist, 1:366-368. S.v. "יכח," by Paul R. Gilchrist, 1:376-377. S.v. "יצא," by Paul R. Gilchrist, 1:393-395. S.v. "ירה," by John E. Hartley, 1:403-405. S.v. "ישר," by Donald J. Wiseman, 1:417-418. S.v. "כון," by John N. Oswalt, 1:433-434. S.v. "לבב," by Andrew Bowling, 1:466-467. S.v. "למד," by Walter C. Kaiser, 1:480. S.v. "נחה," by Leonard J. Coppes, 2:568-569. S.v. "צלח," by John E. Hartley, 2:766. S.v. "צעד," by John E. Hartley, 2:771-772. S.v. "רצון" by William White, 2:859-860. S.v. "שען," by Hermann J. Austel, 2:945-946.

Thompson, Frank Charles, ed. The Thompson Chain-Reference Bible. Indianapolis: B. B. Kirkbride Bible Company, 1964.

Tregelles, Samuel Prideaux, ed. Gesenius' Hebrew and Chaldee Lexicon. Grand Rapids: William B. Eerdmans Publishing Company, 1967.

Vincent, Marvin R. Word Studies in the New Testament. 4 vols. McLean, VA: MacDonald Publishing Company, n.d. Vol. 3: Romans--Corinthians--Ephesians--Philippians--Colossians--Philemon; Vol. 4: The Thessalonian Epistles--The Epistle to the Galatians--The Pastoral Epistles--The Epistle to the Hebrews, by Marvin R. Vincent.

Vine, W. E. An Expository Dictionary of New Testament Words With Their Precise Meanings for English Readers. 4 vols. Old Tappan, NJ: Fleming H. Revell, 1966.

____. Isaiah: Prophecies, Promises, Warnings. Grand Rapids: Zondervan Publishing House, 1969.

Vos, Geerhardus. Biblical Theology. Grand Rapids: William B. Eerdmans Publishing Company, 1966.

Walvoord, John F. Israel in Prophecy. Grand Rapids: Zondervan Publishing House, 1962.

Weiss, G. Christian. The Perfect Will of God. Lincoln: Back to the Bible Publishers, 1950.

Westcott, Brooke Foss, and Fenton John Anthony Hort, eds. The New Testament in the Original Greek. New York: The Macmillan Company, 1928.

Wigram, George V., ed. The Englishman's Greek Concordance to the New Testament. London: Samuel Bagster and Sons, 1903.

Woods, C. Stacey. Some Ways of God. Downers Grove, IL: Intervarsity Press, 1975.

Wuest, Kenneth S. The New Testament: An Expanded Translation. Grand Rapids: William B. Eerdmans Publishing Company, 1961.

_____. Wuest's Word Studies From the Greek New Testament. 3 vols. Grand Rapids: William B. Eerdmans Publishing Company, 1942-54. Vol. 1 (1950-55): Mark--Romans--Galatians--Ephesians and Colossians. Vol. 2 (1942-54): Philippians--Hebrews--The Pastoral Epistles--First Peter--In These Last Days, by Kenneth S. Wuest.

Young, Robert. Analytical Concordance to the Bible. Grand Rapids: William B. Eerdmans Publishing Company, n.d.

PERIODICALS

Allan, John A. "The Will of God in Paul." Expository Times, 72 (December, 1960-May, 1961): 142-145.

Bowers, Margaretta K. "Passive Submission to the Will of God." Pastoral Psychology, 16 (November, 1965): 11-17.

Caird, George B. "The Will of God in the Fourth Gospel." Expository Times, 72 (December, 1960-May, 1961): 115-117.

Gasque, W. Ward. "Is Man's Purpose an Enigma?" Christianity Today, 21 (July 29, 1977): 15-17.

Hartman, Lars. "Your Will be Done on Earth as It is in Heaven." Africa Theological Journal, 11, No. 3 (1982): 209-218.

Jenkins, Jonathan L. "Recognize the Will of the Lord." Dialog (Minneapolis), 22 (Winter, 1983): 64-65.

Monroe, Bill. "Unlocking the Power of Prayer." Fundamentalist Journal, 2, No. 10 (November, 1983): 28-30.

Patterson, Richard D. "Search." Fundamentalist Journal, 2, No. 8 (September, 1983): 34.

Sobosan, Jeffrey G. "The Illusion of Continuity." Journal of Psychology and Theology, 4 (Winter, 1976): 42-46.

Stump, Eleanore, and Norman Kretzmann. "Absolute Simplicity." Faith and Philosophy: Journal of the Society of Christian Philosophers, 2, No. 4 (October, 1985): 353-382.

Taylor, F. J. "The Will of God in the Epistle to the Hebrews." Expository Times, 72 (December, 1960-May,1961): 167-169.

Yancey, Philip. "Finding the Will of God: No Magic Formulas." Christianity Today, 27, No. 14 (September 16, 1983): 24-27.

UNPUBLISHED MATERIALS

Friesen, Garry Lee. "God's Will as it Relates to Decision Making." Th.D. diss., Dallas Theological Seminary, 1978.

McGrew, Benjamin G. Jr. "A Discussion of the 'Call' to the Ministry." Paper presented at Baptist Bible College and Seminary, Clarks Summit, PA. September 21, 1982.

Made in the USA
Charleston, SC
09 November 2015